DEMO FOR EXPORT

by David Pauling

"Democracy is a difficult kind of government. It requires the highest qualities of self-discipline, restraint, a willingness to make commitments and sacrifices for the general interest, and also it requires knowledge."

— John F. Kennedy

 Depot Press Publishing, Tampa, Florida
Phone: 813-885-6794

For additional copies or information contact:
Depot Press Publishing • www.depotpress.com

Design: Joe Tedesco & Kreative Kat Communications, Inc.

All rights reserved. No part of this book may be reproduced or transmitted in any form by any means, electronic or mechanical, including photocopying and recording, or by any information storage or retrieval system, except as may be expressly permitted by the 1976 Copyright Act or in writing by the publisher.

Requests for such permission should be addressed to:
Depot Press Publishing
5018 Tampa West Blvd.
Tampa FL 33634

Copyright © 2004 by David Pauling
ISBN: 0-945827-00-8

Printed in the United States of America

CONTENTS

Chapter	Title	Page
	The Author	VIII
	My Fellow Americans	IX
	Introduction	XII
1	Search for Democracy	1
2	Democracy in Action	9
3	Public Opinion	15
4	Rights, Equality and Equity	23
5	Representative Democracy	31
6	Guaranteed Democracy	39
7	Legislative Government	45
8	Government Officials	53
9	Democracy and Capitalism	59
10	Democracy and Liberty	71
11	Democracy and Power	83
12	Democracy and Opportunity	93
13	Now is the Time	101
14	America	113
15	The End	116
	Epilogue	125

I am deeply indebted to the writings of C. Ivor Brown, Alexis De Tocqueville, E.F. Shumacher, hundreds of journalists and others, whose concepts helped mold my thoughts and guide my words. I am thankful for their efforts on the subject of democracy and hope many others will follow a path that will create "our" America.

The Author

My name is David Pauling, and this book is the result of my 75-year search for an answer to this question: America is a republic, why is it not a democracy? Born in 1928, I grew up in Weirton West Virginia, a steel mill town filled with hard working, hands-on, wealth-creating Americans. In 1943, at age 15, I began my work life as a gandy dancer, laying track on the Pennsylvania Railroad. At 16, I went into the local steel mill, forging 8-inch artillery shells. At 17, I dropped out of high school and enlisted in the U.S. Marines. Eight years and two wars later, I returned to civilian life as a millwright and then as a structural ironworker.

Determined to find a better way, I started educating myself by reading every book, newspaper and magazine I could find. Like Diogenes cynical search for an honest man, I went in search of the-truth, a lifelong struggle against life's everyday realities.

At age twenty-nine I went into sales — travelling throughout the USA, Europe, and the Far East exposed me to many other cultures and political systems-- my earnings ultimately provided me with the ways and means to start my own structural steel fabricating business. In 1989 an industrial accident forced me into an early retirement. In 1990 I enrolled in St Petersburg Junior College. Graduating with honors I went on to the University of South Florida, earning a BA in Interdisciplinary Social Science.

Then, on December 27, 2003, my daughter delivered Jessica, my only grandchild. On the day she was born — our America is engaged in another unnecessary war that robs us of our dignity and steals from our national treasury — her share of the current seven trillion-dollar national debt was $23,871... and that's not right, and it's certainly not fair. Soon I will be gone, and she will be in charge of my heritage, taking what I have done and making it better, looking at what I have not done and doing something about it.

My fellow Americans…

Because both past and present Republican and Democratic Administrations are obviously in bed with Wall Street lobbyists, I am having a hard time telling one bought and paid for Republican from another bought and paid for Democrat. So, let's call all of them "Republicrats" and ask, Why are We, the People, allowing them to forever cut taxes for their rich friends and then borrow billions upon billions of dollars against our children's future?

From the first George W. from Mount Vernon, Virginia, to the present George W. from Crawford Texas, we have blindly served and silently suffered under these never-ending rule-by-wealth regimes, some 228 years of promises made that are seldom, if ever, kept. The answers to their lies, are not more lies. It is and must always be the truth that we need that we don't want to hear.

The Federal budget is completely out of control. The national debt, already over seven-trillion dollars, is currently increasing by nearly two-billion dollars each and every day — the annual interest payment alone, will increase this federal debt by nearly four-hundred billion dollars. In just the last thirty-four years, Wall Street has accumulated a five-trillion dollar international trade deficit. To this known amount of public debt and self-serving fiscal irresponsibility, you should also become aware of a well-hidden forty-six-trillion dollar secret — an unfunded government liability to Social Security, Medicare and Federal Retirement Programs.

Here and now, it is time to stop this Republicratic mantra of empire building — spending money they don't have on special interest projects we don't need and on wars they can't win. A methodology of deficit spending that is in fact a weird form of secretly financing incumbent politicians.

My fellow Americans

In the 1950's, then President Dwight Eisenhower warned us of the catastrophic results of continuing a nationalized military-industrial mentality. The Republicrats, of course, ignored his warning and we are now living with the consequences — a shortsighted self-serving rule by the power of confiscated wealth. The best government that money can buy, creating one catastrophe after another.

Their Korean War has become a fifty-year old albatross. Vietnam was a political disaster, and our military activities in Panama and Nicaragua deserve better explanations than were ever offered. And now through waste, chaos, and cronyism, we have an ever-growing $200 billion mess in Afghanistan and Iraq.

All of these roads to taxpayer hell were paved with pre-emptive political rhetoric and too many dead Americans. While the overall cure is what this book is all about, as a first dose of reality let's make it illegal to profit on manufacturing the tools of war.

From this day forward, We, the People, need to start asking the most basic of all questions: Whose land is this? My fellow Americans, at one time, we at least thought this was our America, but 25,000 Wall Street lobbyists in our nation's capital have highjacked our political process. Their self-serving vision of a One-World economy is continually chipping away at our individual freedoms and personal prosperity.

Through our current imperialistic presidency and the Patriot Act, our rights to "liberty and justice for all" are rapidly disappearing. From Reagan, through Bush, Clinton, and now Bush W., this nation's environmental laws, tax laws, securities laws, and trade laws are being continually rewritten-- gutted to directly benefit the Wall Street robber barons whose only goals are to benefit themselves.

My fellow Americans

We can no longer ignore the truth. Fifteen million highly qualified American craftsmen can't find a decent job. Thirty-five million are mired in poverty. Forty-five million of the working poor can't afford health insurance.

Contributing to these problems our nation's antiquated school systems are delivering little more than additional bodies to die in unnecessary wars, or fail to survive in today's high tech world. And these are only some of the many failures of this nation's perverse political doctrine — a plutocracy of greed, a culture of rule by confiscated wealth, an unnecessary rich that created and is now expanding our unwanted poor.

If indeed we are the world's champions of "liberty and justice for all," is it not time to practice what we preach? Is it not time for all of us to take one step forward, and leave none of us behind?

Here and now, I am asking you to prove your patriotism. All you have to do is vote. If each and every one of us will exercise this Constitutional right it will send a warning to all politicians, telling them We, the People, are the majority and we will be heard. Or you will be replaced.

My fellow Americans, we are standing in the footprints of every dead American who in their time did what had to be done to preserve the original promise of "We, the People." I now ask you to do no less. You and I working together can, and we must, turn this Republic of States into a Democracy of Human Beings?

INTRODUCTION

This treatise is my personal view as a citizen of the plutocratic republic called the United States of America. Wait a minute! America is a democracy, isn't it? If you ask most Americans this question they'll say yes, of course we're a democracy. But the truthful answer is no, for democracy in America is only an illusion.

In the beginning, when America first came into being, We, the People, relied upon the volunteer leadership of the better-educated slaveholders and property owners to form what we thought would be our government. But now, this nation is being endlessly spoiled and wasted by their successors, a symbiotic brotherhood of Wall Street profiteers and their Washington Republicrats.

Honesty, integrity, and truth have become rare qualities in both local and national political office. The confiscation of wealth, through creative economic schemes and preferential tax concessions for the already wealthy, has become the primary focus of their government. There is widespread uncertainty as to what can be done to get this nation back on track, to finally deliver on its 228 year old promise of "liberty and justice for all".

While this nation has long called itself the guardian of all free people, there is just cause to fear that our own freedoms are being totally undermined. On a worldwide basis we are continually called upon to defend the human rights and ideals of democracy… while here at home the Republicrats conceal their non-existence. The truth is, their government could never convince us to fight and die for the ideals of Wall Street profiteers. Yet that is exactly what they order us to do.

Even in their most casual mention of the term democracy, this nation's managers, (I cannot call them leaders) are pur-

Introduction

posely dividing us and preventing our unity. What we think is our America has become Wall Street's land of greed, a home for their depraved indifference to the rights of We, the People.

Here and now, we need to stop, look, and listen! To reclaim our America we must understand that our need for a real democracy requires that we also learn the ways and means of our-creation of new wealth vs. their-confiscation of our-productivity.

The truth is, new wealth can only be created by nature and by human interaction with these raw materials. First and foremost, this nation's natural resources must be nurtured, shared, defended by all, and owned by none. And all that is enhanced by the added value of human effort (the origin of new wealth) must be identified with an individual's right of creative ownership.

We, the People, long denied equitable compensation for our hands-on contribution to increasing the value of our nation's resources, have until now relied upon a system of wages and welfare, without the dignity of ownership. This incorporate-master vs. wage-slave mentality has fostered an immense inequality among equals, leaving the new-wealth creating worker forever dependent — and the totally dependent capitalists forever wealthier.

Here and now, every American, in the cause of our-humanity before their-profit, must abandon this plutocracy of rule by wealth. To all registered, unregistered and non-voting Americans — you may dispute the priority I place upon the value of democracy, but it is better to argue about strong principles than to endure wage-slave servitude — together we can build our-America.

CHAPTER 1
SEARCH FOR DEMOCRACY

> *Democracy is about what is best in all-human relationships.*

Here it is time to ask: Why is it thieves of every kind are always planning a way to become rich without effort, by taking wealth created by another? And the answer is, because our apathy, naiveté and ignorance let it happen. The use of threat or strength to enforce confiscation and oppression, as practiced by all thieves, bullies and those who would be king, has been with us since the recorded beginnings of humanity.

The truth is, despite America's vast resources and what should be an unlimited opportunity for every citizen, we find our quality of life continually jeopardized by both corporate and government managers, singularly focused on their profit before our humanity. When an individual works to create new wealth, and someone more powerful takes all they can steal, is the end result of bullies or kings any different?

In "The Law," (1850) Frederic Bastiat wrote, "Man can live and satisfy his wants only by ceaseless labor; by the ceaseless application of his facilities to natural resources. This process is the origin of property. But it is also true that a man may live and satisfy his wants by seizing and consuming the products of the labors of others. This process is the origin of plunder."

Civilized history reveals that every advancement made by humankind, though achieved by the efforts of all, is invariably manipulated to benefit only a few. Even democracy, a self-governing system meant to free all the people, has been diverted to another purpose. This wonderful inheritance, intended for improvement by each generation, requires an effort that goes far beyond just taking the trouble to be born.

Our forefathers promised a more humane equality, with "liberty and justice for all." We are told to believe that they're already ours. Do you believe they are? Think about that for a minute, and then reflect on what has become their-government's primary objective — world power and corporate profit.

While Washington Republicrats have long preached a tale of democracy, it is in fact a plutocracy, an absolute rule by the power of wealth. Using the best government that money can buy to enforce its confiscation, Wall Street has assumed full control of our nation. Yet We, the People, naively continue referring to an illusion called democracy.

While the sound of the word democracy may provide a comforting (though false) sense of pleasure, there is just cause to ask: What do we mean by democracy? Are the democratic rights to "life, liberty and the pursuit of happiness" for all? Or, for only those who can afford them?

Something is Wrong

Because we are now media conditioned to be far more concerned about material things than we are about thoughts, Wall Street's right of confiscation has even limited our right of inquisition. Their questions to Washington Republicrats are answered with immediate action. Our questions are not even heard. The wealthy are all powerful and hypocrisy is the only measure of their every action, word or deed. Brazenly they connive, in order to possess and covet all that can be made from every thought, product or process, without any concern about the other guy.

These carefully orchestrated events continually divide us into ever narrowing cultural values and social class identities, intentionally destroying our natural desire for common purpose, making a real democracy in our America seem a long way off.

The truth is, Americans are not a homogeneous people in nationality or race. We most certainly are not, as many have tried to declare, a melting pot. We are instead a salad bowl of distinct individuals that can mix and match into unlimited combinations of wonderful new capabilities. Truly enriched by these different cultural and ethnic origins, we must search for and find ways to unify our national objectives, but not by forgetting our pride as unique individuals.

Caution. Even small losses of our already limited individual rights, can become a terrifying weapon. For example, allowing loose or variable government actions like The Patriot Act, to covertly limit our individual rights, may actually encourage some lunatic's attempt at dictatorial control. If you truly want democracy, you must first be able to find it and define it, and once you possess it you must prepare yourself to protect and defend it forever.

Be reminded — a small group of people banding together in defiance of all that confronted them is what provided our nation's starting point. A forced religion, unfair taxes, and an arrogant king were important considerations in this nation's first Declaration of Independence. This exuberant cry for freedom, coupled with a frontier advantage and a common enemy, created an instant unity among these radical individualists, forging a collective free will that formed our beginning.

Almost from day one however, even as our self-determination grew stronger, we allowed the rich and powerful to abuse this newly created nation. With now very well practiced ease, they have covertly replaced our original spark of unity for common purpose with too much greed, and too little tolerance for the weaker members of our society.

The possibilities of a seemingly unlimited territory constantly added to ever changing rules, and we did little to guarantee the preservation of the Declaration's original ideals. If we can now whittle away this materialistic confusion our America could become what it should have been in the first place, a democracy — a cooperative free will of We, the People, nurturing a national sense of the common good, and a self-imposed commitment of our individual responsibility. With a true democracy in place, a natural leadership would swiftly emerge, truly representative of the people it intended to serve.

Today we find ourselves living in an age of ever-advancing technology, where everyone should be allowed to explore the infinite possibilities of success for all. Never in our history was there a time more ripe, or the need more obvious, for an open discussion on the subjects of individual rights and economic parity. Yet few people will speak out.

The truth is, America's so-called government of, by, and for, the people is totally controlled by Wall Street lobbyists through their bought and paid-for Washington Republicrats. Even as individuals few of them can declare democracy is their intent, for all are materialistically infected, some far more than others.

Turn to any newspaper, listen to any commentator, and be aware that the truth is being distorted to sell us some new corporate media version of the same old tune, favoring Wall Street profit over our humanity. Seldom if ever mentioned, except when presented as a patriotic showcase to an outside world — Democracy, is for export only.

Because this search for democracy is focused on our humanity as opposed to their profit, we need to ask the Republicrats and ourselves, What national purpose is served by American blood being shed to preemptively invade or occupy another foreign land, under a pretext of installing a democracy?

Who is fooling whom? If we do not have democracy in America, how is it that we can so generously offer it for export to so many others? Perhaps it may even be time to ask: Who is this powerful stranger we call government?

The truth is…

From this point forward, the answers to all questions will require an open mind and a personal commitment to "liberty and justice for all". Therefore, to actually achieve democracy, this magnificent idea for which we are willing to die, we will have to first agree on what this word really means to us as individuals.

Ask two teachers and one lawyer, two engineers and one cafe waitress, two construction workers and one partisan politician, and any one of the thirty-five million Americans who now live in poverty, and you will have at least ten different definitions for what the ideals of democracy represent. It really does not help us to talk of "making the world safe for democracy," when any ten Americans, supplying ten different answers, have no idea what this statement really means.

Our misunderstanding and confusion is being generated by this nation's vastly under-funded educational system, where most Americans are taught to read but are not taught to "think outside the box." Yet, it is always us, the huddled masses, who must constantly stand ready to create new wealth, pay our taxes, and fight for the very principles of individual freedom that our nation's managers keep trying to take away.

Now ignored by self-serving politicians, and endlessly misinformed by cynical commentators, we are media conditioned to accept their fair and balanced versions of vague and nothing — as great and wonderful. Democracy, a permanent cure for the world's human inequities, has become their spin-doctored Judas goat, leading us to slaughter.

Continually luring us into their trap, we are forever promised their new pathways to our salvation. Blinded by false purpose and patriotic rhetoric, we have placed our faith and trust in their self-serving monumental creations.

We, the hands-on, wealth-creating, everyday Americans have paid for New Deals, Great Societies, Moral Majorities, trickle down economics, and trickle up tax cuts for the rich. In the dawning light of truth and reality we have all seen these towering hopes fall to the ground. There are many reasons for failure — incessant greed, petty jealousies, pure arrogance. and false ambitions not being the least of them.

If the First Amendment to the U.S. Constitution means anything, it means the public has a right to know the truth. Our ability to function as citizens depends on a free-flow of information between our leaders and our selves.

But the truth is… our continuing apathy and indifference concerning Washington scandals and Wall Street fraud has actually encouraged them to brazenly flaunt their insatiable desire for ever more wealth and greater power. Their thinking is blatantly obvious. When we don't care what happens to the other guy, the bully takes it all. Left uncorrected, this attitude will prove fatal to what we think is our America.

Because democracy in our America is now virtually inoperative, its complete elimination is an ominous threat to our very existence. It is time to decide if we actually want democracy as our governing philosophy. Once we are resolved, the government must abide by what we demand.

Fixing the Problem

At this point we need to stop, take a deep breath, and prepare ourselves for an adventure — a journey into the unknown, with many pitfalls that must be overcome. Democracy, like all really big ideas, begins with high ideals and goals that are pictured far beyond the realm of actual human experience. Though we may get smart enough to understand the truth, truth with integrity may be difficult to find. If we do not pay close attention to our task, patient capitalists and self-serving Republicrats can easily divert our efforts toward failure.

But even democracy cannot save us if we have only a vague notion of what it's all about. The current war-like state of the nation's affairs demands a remedy that must come from a majority of the individuals who make up the nation, not from Wall Street.

First and foremost, We, the People, must reclaim our free will, value the common good, and accept our share of individual responsibility. We must take a personal stand on all issues that will address civic, economic, and political equality, lest apathy, indifference, and mindless servitude become the only surviving measures of our existence.

For the record, this treatise is only meant to analyze, define and present the idea called democracy — so you may choose to be for it, or against it. At least for the moment, the right of choice is still available. But soon, you may have to choose it, or you will lose it.

CHAPTER 2

DEMOCRACY IN ACTION

> *The most dastardly of all crimes against democrac is apathy.*

We drown our morality in ritualistic law, encase our values in social weakness, and then we display complete political apathy. The who, what, when, where, why, and how of a nation's governing philosophy is rarely understood. To remedy this defect in our national thinking, we need to define the words that connect a nation to its people and its people to their power.

At present, the most equitable of all known governing philosophies is democracy. By its deference to the rights of the majority, it provides a natural balance between the source and use of power. This word is a combination of two Greek words, demos, meaning "the people," and kratia, meaning "power." Therefore, democracy, as we will use the word, is the people's power.

For contrast, the Greeks have also provided a definition of our current governing system: a plutocracy. Plutos meaning "wealth" and kratia, meaning "power," hence, rule by the power of wealth.

The meanings of other Greek-based words can sometimes complicate the process of identifying who is in command. As an example: Aristocracy, the "best men's power," implies a question of, "best in what?" The Greeks, who first employed the word, used it as a general term meaning best in character and brain. The European use is generally best by birth, while the American use is best by wealth.

In America there is an often-accepted belief that any superiority of character and brain is really more a matter of who you know, rather than what you know. Where you go to school is often more important than your grades or your class standing. Access to positions of power, in business and politics, are frequently based more on brown noses and blue blood than on an individual's ability to actually do the job.

In the beginning...

Originally, this nation's governing system was aligned with centuries old long-standing rules of common law and the Rite-of-Kings. This established the founder's right to restrict individuality and display strength as was necessary to maintain the historical status quo and control the public at large.

Thus, any government that achieves and maintains control of the masses can call itself any name it chooses. It can even call itself a democracy, but the word so used, means nothing. For between the public's tolerance of an absolute ruling potentate, and our resolve that the machinery of government must act for the common good, there is an area called apathy, a particularly destructive force within our pretended democracy.

Despite the obvious problem of this apathy that we must overcome, the term democracy, as will be used throughout this treatise, will mean "the people's power" is voluntarily transferred to elected representatives and charged to act on our behalf. But be aware, even this perfectly plain statement has a concealed double meaning.

Politicians, as custodians of our individual power, aspire to what we think of as a limited term of office. But once elected, they are free to rule the roost. Through readily available financial support from special interests, they can easily establish a permanent hold on what we thought was only a temporary transfer. They can, and often do approve laws that the majority may not approve of at all.

Thus, every defective politician we have is simply the result of us, the apathetic majority of irresponsible voters. Think about it… if we are not willing to check on them, Washington and Wall Street will gladly keep our power and continue using it as their own.

America's Republicrats have thereby become totally misrepresentative of the people's rights. Though this nation's government maintains an appearance of being based on majority choice rather than rule by force, Wall Street tyranny driven by old-fashioned greed is the reality.

Once before in American history we found ourselves under an oppressive tyranny. A British king that abused his colonists to a point of resentment by a few and irritation by many. The Boston Tea Party, one of several public demonstrations that led to a revolution, provides one colorful image of what we thought was supposed to become a democracy.

This first American revolution was not a vague or ill-defined craving for national independence. It was the result of mature reasoning and a hunger for individual freedom. There was no passionate cry of anarchy for the sake of anarchy. Our course of action was simply a desire for self-government, the goal We, the People, did not achieve.

Here and now, we must once more take time for a serious consideration of viable alternatives to the economic tyranny that has control of our America. Unknowingly, we have allowed ourselves to be endlessly misled into accepting their rule by the power of the confiscated wealth they are actually taking from us.

We find ourselves in a high state of social despair, completely surrounded by economic dishonesty and political confusion. This situation requires that we stop here to identify the nature and meaning of where and how power accumulates within any human assemblage.

The solution pivots on our ability to isolate a recognizable sovereign, the person or group of persons who will hold our power and lead the nation. This individual, or group of individuals found and identified, will from this point on be referred to as our Legal Sovereign.

Headed by the president, elected and appointed government officials now fill this role as America's Legal Sovereign. They are the users of the nation's power, for good or evil, but they are not the actual sources of power. For behind this Legal Sovereign there is an Ultimate Sovereign, the nation's citizenry, who through the power of their vote can exercise its voice in support, opposition, or passive submission.

Unfortunately, history has shown that every Legal Sovereign is somehow always charged with a secretive inner impulse to continually reduce or even eliminate the power of their Ultimate Sovereigns. Eventually this impulse will invariably grow into dreams of dominion and empire. Is this our nation's current state of affairs?

Financed by Wall Street's capitalists, the American version of this impulse now maintains an absolute plutocracy, a Legal Sovereign with an insatiable hunger for ever-more confiscated wealth and worldly power. As a direct result, these private interest capitalists are now completely free to use their confiscated wealth to run the machinery of their government as they please. Making themselves ever more rich and powerful, they are at liberty, by the laws they can ordain, to violate our rights at will, and thereby serve only their own ambitions. Allowed by We, the People, an apathetic and docile electorate, this is the critical defect in America's existing governing system.

We must change

When any Legal Sovereign chooses to forget the rights of its Ultimate Sovereign, an obvious rift should naturally occur. This complete ignoring of the majority's voice could ultimately become the motivation needed to finally institute a real democracy in what could be our America.

Be reminded, that in any nation that would have democracy as its governing philosophy, the public's opinion must never be silent or even vague. It must be openly stated by each individual, and demonstrated in every national activity. "The tree of liberty must be refreshed from time to time with the blood of patriots and tyrants. It is the natural manure." (Thomas Jefferson)

To achieve democracy in what could be our America, we can and we must use our right to vote, and thereby assert our right to direct our government to do our bidding. When common purpose is combined with the free will of a well-informed majority of its citizens, democracy will simply happen. It is actually that easy.

There are, however, many steps that must be climbed before the majority can actually attain this goal. Democracy can only be reached when the free will of all the people is combined, and then protected and served by its elected government.

There are many obvious differences between government of,

by, and for the people and a government that rules by force and confiscation. Only a clearly focused effort toward understanding these critical differences can help us resolve the problem and give content and real meaning to that frequently abused word, democracy.

Fortunately, there is a tremor of hope now being felt throughout the land, a rapidly increasing disgust coming from deep within the people's majority. All Washington Republicrats had best remind themselves that a nation can never remain strong if the support from its people grows weak.

No government has ever been conceived that can turn a community of disgusted and indifferent citizens into an active and energetic people. Only democracy in action can be the foundation of a new America that is for all the people. Perhaps now may be the time for every one of us to stand up and shout, "I'm mad as hell, and I'm not going to take it any more!"

CHAPTER 3

PUBLIC OPINION

> *The strength of this nation is We the People.*

As we have seen, democracy can only happen when there is a mutual agreement between the Legal Sovereign and its Ultimate Sovereign. As well, the people are best served when the public's opinion is both heard and felt by the nation's Legal Sovereign.

But, what truly constitutes public opinion? When is our individual opinion formed? How does it grow? Can what we say or do really have an effect on what is happening in Washington, or on Wall Street?

Historically, the American people are naturally traditional, generally tolerant, and passively indifferent beings who nearly always prefer to avoid trouble and disagreement. Unfortunately, our nation's managers have interpreted this innate desire for a peaceful co-existence as a weakness in our character.

As a result, the public's opinion is continually manipulated by the incorporate media to react like Pavlov's dogs, from flag-waving patriotism, celebrity trials, religious pandering, and flaunting displays of the lavish lifestyles of the rich and famous. The truth is nowhere to be found.

This media-conditioned indifference to political, economic, and social class reality has worked directly against our own well being, freeing the Republicrats to further weaken the value of the public's opinion. And, unless you consciously decide to start resisting, and thereby make a difference, their methods are not going to change.

One truth that does await every one of us, is the disappointment that comes from thinking we will accept the truth when it is told. For we are a nation of believers, and thereby politicians and capitalists can get away with anything, for our civic duty, like our bedroom door, remains tightly closed. We will not even admit a problem exists until it is ready to destroy us.

Please take the time to stop and carefully consider these two statements: 1) The truth we need is almost never what we want to hear. 2) While the truth may also be stated as a belief, the opposite is not possible.

If you are now ready to at least consider the truth, the confiscation and distribution of the nation's natural resources will provide our starting point. Should we question the incongruity of who should have ownership? The plutocratic system we have is continually polluting the relatively free air and water we require for survival by contaminating it with toxic waste, from the products that are being processed from the confiscated earth we stand upon. Of course, We, the People, will then pay to clean up their mess.

The truth is, we need to restore the clean environment our forefathers enjoyed. They were able to breathe a fresh and clean air that smelled of freedom and justice as they created a nation that began with greatness. But materialistic greed is now fouling every aspect of nature, and this nation's greatness is being diminished in direct proportion to the collapse of our environment.

A second case of real concern is our national defense requirements vs. military weapon manufacturers. What standard of human morality was used in granting commercial captains of industry the exclusive right to all they can grab? Washington Republicrats have made it perfectly legal for Wall Street to acquire and hoard all the profits they can skim off from any product or service, and they can hardly be expected to forego the creaming from such a plentiful profit source as war tool production. This is a major case of approved exploitation; special interests defining the nation's need to defend itself, and their government blatantly allowing the capitalists to rape it for private profit and personal gain.

While these war tool manufacturers are abusing the national necessity for defense, making wage-slaves of the defended (their employees) and excessive profits for absentee, frequently foreign stockholders, is it proper that military service personnel face great danger or even death for what amounts to a minimum wage? The artistry of Wall Street economics teaches that shortages mean high prices and big profits. That what has caused these shortages is an ongoing series of unjustified preemptive wars, in which young Americans must fight and die is of no concern.

The truth is, there are too many of these highly questionable political-economic relationships in every level of this nation's government. Wall Street scandals, insider trading, corporate tax cheating, and endless demands for taxpayer bailouts of privately owned America have become daily events.

Conditioned by this constant exposure to cronyism and corruption, too many Americans who would normally go out of their way to avoid hurting anyone, will now not hesitate to lie, steal, or cheat because it's the only way to win. I will not explore the mental or moral images being transmitted to the nation's youth by these public displays of obviously criminal activities.

Unfortunately, humankind has a long-standing bad habit of consistently adhering to its ritualistic customs, distorted cultural values, and the roots of passive submissive consent that produces the public opinion, which then becomes deeply set by rampant combinations of illogical faiths and illegal practices, whose origins, interpretations and misapplications, would require more than this over-long sentence, this humble volume or an entire encyclopedic analysis could ever determine.

History has, however, proven that public opinion can change. Eventually logic and reason can prevail, and humanity will take a small step toward its own survival. Look at the advancements that have occurred in fairly modern times. We have completely stopped the practice of feeding Christians to the lions. As another sign of human concern, some of the oven operators from Hitler's Germany were actually prosecuted. Fettered slavery, indentured servitude, and debtor prisons are now comparatively rare.

Logic and reason, at least in these few instances, seems to have prevailed. Someday, logic may even make us pause to consider releasing all subservient wage-slaves and canceling all wars, our disgusting habit of butchering people who happen to have a different belief than our own.

The truth is, regardless of the action or issue, the really decisive power of public opinion can only occur when there is a majority agreement made up of the people's free will. No truly free human being will eagerly fight for just any god, any country, or any cause that is not also his own. Our progressively downward spiral of costly experiments in Korea, Vietnam, Afghanistan, and now Iraq come to mind.

On the other hand, we do have one comparatively recent positive experience to build upon. The first advocates of racial equality in America were regarded as rebellious malcontents and disruptive do-gooders. After years of public contempt, physical abuse, and even criminal prosecution, their views eventually became respectable and some of their immediate demands were passed into law and public acceptance. Some extremists, seeking reparations, still expound upon this injustice.

While the truth is almost always an indigestible commodity, a determined individual or a group that brings forward an idea whose time has come, can indeed weave a new strand of thought into the texture of our national cloth. Indeed, if we prepare ourselves to face ridicule and rejection, even this humble appeal for democracy, (if supported by the people,) could ultimately become the public's opinion. Would you care to support the idea of a real democracy in what could be our-America?

Out of Control

A major tragedy in America is the subliminal messages being conveyed to the general public by the Wall Street controlled media through their talking heads of misinformation — endless distortions of the truth we need that can so easily divert and thus control the public's opinion.

Merely distorting the truth can itself become a brainwashing tool of power when manipulated by the government, the corporate media or who-ever comes along. Through intensive persuasion and repetition posturing performers can easily claim a fair and balanced presentation of the news, which it usually turns out is only a different version of Wall Street's plutocratic propaganda.

Despite our individual ability to reason and resolve, any psychologist who has studied the effect of commercial advertising realizes the tremendous hypnotic power of continual repetition. If their media keeps telling the same story, day after day, even those who at first resist or have doubts will eventually begin to believe. I do not intend to overly pursue this point, but we should understand the potential dangers of repeated lies, a severe detriment to every facet of the democracy that we seek.

Never forget that faked news or even a significant silence can create a false belief that is capable of swaying the masses, the lack of weapons of mass destruction in Iraq is an excellent example. A truly free press, reporting only the truth, could provide new goals and more accurate objectives, and this in turn could become the foundation of a new public opinion upon which a real democracy could be established in our America.

Here it is important to note that our individual opinion is initially inherited from family and cultural exposure during our early formative years. This collective, (though sometimes narrow,) source molds our tastes and traditions while external forces, like education, job contacts, personal relations, and of course media distortion, can easily and effectively alter our later values.

The truth is, public opinion is never complete or absolute, for it is merely a current collage of our needs, wants, fears, hopes, desires, and moral judgements. In times of emergency, it can create a national consensus of purposeful cooperation, over-riding all individual needs, focusing only on the priority that demands a justifiable immediate action, i.e., our successful response to the Japanese attack on Pearl Harbor. Or, our initial response to 9-11, later contaminated by lies, distortion and misinformation to achieve a different objective.

Change is Good

In a true democracy however, our government would naturally value and utilize the majority's opinion in its division and distribution of political power to protect and serve We, the People. Few, if any, of the nation's activities could then become restrictive towards this balance, and the end result would consistently support our common needs.

From this it must be said, as this nation's Ultimate Sovereign, we have both an individual and collective obligation to remain alert and ready to use our right to call the government to account when it fails to deliver our needs.

At present, it is of course the affluent that can easily affect and thus control the public's opinion and hence, the nation's affairs. Democracy in America will happen, as soon as the public's opinion ceases to be tolerant of this self-anointing plutocracy.

The people will then, by active resolution, demand that all power be returned to this nation's Ultimate Sovereigns — We, the People.

The Republicrats, for obvious reasons, will mightily resist this radical truth and it is here where the bottleneck begins.

Accepting the principles of democracy, and thereby exercising the power of public opinion as the ideal, means there will be no reason for denying the law-abiding citizen full entitlement and possession of all their freedoms and their rights to the values of human dignity.

Democracy, to be genuine, must start with a firm foundation and a doctrine of equitable equality where everyone is equal under the law, and not with the notion that some, by reasons of their equity, are more equal than others.

Thus, if We, the People, can agree to this pursuit of democracy, the public's opinion can quickly become the public policy. At that point there would be a cry for change in the Legal Sovereign's performance, and the American people, as the nation's Ultimate Sovereign, will then demand democracy — a government of the people, by the people, and for the people, as we thought was originally intended.

Fortunately, We, the People, are uniquely capable of deciding the final result of this examination of democracy. My continuing purpose is to simply state the truth that will allow the reader to reach an informed and decisive conclusion. To this end, we need to keep trying to discover what democracy could mean to all the people, if we decide it's what we really need.

So far the meaning of words and purposeful reason in expression of the public opinion has been our only conclusion. To have a democracy, we must simply choose between remaining a subservient nobody, or becoming an individual somebody. It's actually that easy.

CHAPTER 4
RIGHTS, EQUALITY and EQUITY

> *Men cannot remain forever unequal upon a single point if he is equal on all others.*

Those who would promote democracy cry out, "All are created equal." What precisely does this mean? To say that all are equal is to also imply that all are alike and that is simply not possible. Each and every one of us are provided with varying amounts of differing physical and psychological qualities that assure an infinite "salad bowl" of possibilities. The truth is, it has taken all kinds of people to make America great, and there is no use closing our eyes to their existence.

Likewise, it is ludicrous to assert the equality of all, arguing not the equality of rights but rather the equality of content. Some have argued that all property possessed by the few should be divided among the many on some abstract principle of democratic equality. But this cannot be, for the truth is, we live in a Republic, under Republicratic rules, where democracy is nowhere to be found..

In The Declaration of Independence, Thomas Jefferson wrote, "We hold these truths to be self-evident, that all men are created equal, that they are endowed by their Creator with certain inalienable Rights, that among these are Life, Liberty and the Pursuit of Happiness. That to secure these rights, Governments are instituted among men, deriving their just powers from the consent of the governed." These often repeated assertions were neither borne out by recorded history, nor are they present in current government practices.

To correct the potential abuse of this deficiency Jefferson added: "That whenever any Form of Government becomes destructive of these ends, it is the Right of the People to alter or abolish it, and to institute new Government, laying its foundation on such principles and organizing its powers in such form, as to them shall seem most likely to affect their safety and happiness."

Thus, if a true democracy were to become our America's governing philosophy, it would be the start of something new and different, an equitable human equality, a logical basis for a natural morality in our lives. In this way it is somewhat like a religion, in that it is a faith based on humanity and democracy as one entity.

Those who believe America ought to be a democracy will unflinchingly accept this tenet as it stands. Those who would oppose any change to the status quo will go to great lengths to assure its failure.

To every American I ask, Do you believe God allowed humankind to come into being, only to be eternally committed to the miseries of master and slave relationships? Assuming the prime directive of our earthly humanity is to continually seek our own perfection, it needs to be asked: How much longer must we accept a subservient role? Why should we live in an obviously imperfect world when a perfect balance of political, economic, and social democracy can be so easily achieved? Should we passively allow our individual rights to be legislatively limited in any way? , should we instead, freely pursue equitable and humane values? Democracy will naturally provide the answers, but only when we continuously ask the right questions.

Filling the Void

To actually achieve democracy in our America, we will all need to learn far more than just the basic meaning of selected words, for there is also the feelings and attitudes that some words can evoke. Somehow, every one of us must learn and understand the absolute power of no, as well as yes. For only then can we rightfully accept or reject all that comes before us.

At present, we have an inequitable political system. We, the People, pay for everything, but get very little in return. We have an inequitable economic system. When there is more month than there is money, we get scared, perplexed and angry, but our apathy keeps us trapped in their-system. The truth is, we need what we don't have, a political, economic, and social democracy that works for us.

To fill this void in ourselves, we will need to search for and acquire new skills and abilities that will enhance both our personal choices and common objectives, not destroy them. In short, we need to find and accept the truth that would flow naturally from open and honest relationships, the missing qualities in our present social, economic and political systems.

The truth is, when we accept any limitation on our right to an equitable human equality; we make ourselves the natural victim of the more powerful. Mislead by false promises, down secret roads that can only end in eternal servitude, the practice of allowing the few to take more than they need has produced an absurd right to be excessively rich by making someone else excessively poor. It is this purposely restrictive Republicratic law-making that is allowing these distortions.

The natural right to a more equitable form of human of equality must belong to every man and woman. This point needs to be clearly established and firmly accepted in a comparative light of general utility and common happiness. If all believers and practitioners of democracy would limit their credo to this one claim, we could socially remain on politically practical and economically even ground.

The nation's Republicrats however, cannot leave anything alone that does not provide them with greater power. In their hands, any doctrine of individual rights creates an automatic demand for a sequence of controlling legal restrictions that have been used by every thief, king, or prelate who would capture and confine the free activities of the human spirit in service to the chosen few.

Always it is a question of whose version of equality should we pursue? Many have pronounced that all are born equal and cannot be made unequal. Yet this nation's plutocrats have successfully convinced us we are born unequal and should always be kept that way. But it must be asked, how did they assume the power to decide which child should be born with a silver spoon, while another is born to a life of abject poverty?

Their argument contends that the whole concept of equality is man made and they allow it because it only implies (but doesn't have to deliver,) happiness for all. Should our demands for an equitable human equality become an impediment to their self-serving causes, then rights or no rights, it is time for their government to legally disallow it.

By now it should be getting obvious: the only governing philosophy that can actually deliver "life, liberty and the pursuit of happiness" is democracy. Through an exercise of our free will power of Ultimate Sovereignty, in every public and private action, its principles of equitable equality will naturally keep us openly unified, and yet freely independent of each other.

Democracy would thus resolve every dilemma by establishing truly fair and balanced values for all that are independent of spirit, and this quality is a demanded requirement of those who would guide the nation. The voice of the people is not infallible, but it is the surest guide to our common welfare.

By simply doing what must be done, democracy will constantly assure that opportunity for all goes into every action. It demands the nation's leadership agree to treat everyone alike. Not because we are really alike, but because the divisive standards of separation or comparison among individuals become impossible among millions.

Thus, a more equitable form of human equality is the only way to get on with practical politics in America. Actually, some minor philosophical points of democracy may prove unworkable, but its self-leveling action will always work when put into full operation.

Social Equality vs. Economic Equity

Here, we must examine the conflicting differences between social equality and economic equity. The comparison may seem hard and involved, but an example will make it plain. Equality under existing law implies that each of us be treated as equals. But as equity alters the circumstances of each case, this theory of human equality can lead to unfairness in individual cases.

For example: When equality under the law fails to properly address justice, equity becomes the determining factor. Two accused defendants equally innocent or guilty of like crimes may be legally treated unequally, when based only upon the individual's ability to buy and pay for varying levels of available lawyer skill. While one of the accused may be found guilty and go to jail for life, the other may be declared innocent and end up totally free. Equity not equality decides the difference.

If all you want from your existence is personal comfort and a general well being, this can be obtained by simply diverting your moral and intellectual activities to this purpose. On the other hand, choosing democracy requires that we work on behalf of the nation as well as our selves. This will require a harmony and balance that can only flow from openness instead of secrecy, peace instead of war, and minor personal vices instead of major corporate crimes. These directly opposing comparisons demand our individual consideration of something far greater than the inequitable equality we have.

Common prosperity can only flow naturally from an open society that does not attempt control of man by purposely creating laws (or sins) to limit what comes naturally. Only when their government removes its priority on a worldly pursuit of international power, and confines itself to actions that insure the greatest enjoyment and least misery for its citizenry, will the value of our humanity take center stage.

The truth is, We, the people, will have democracy when we simply decide to accept a more equitable form of human equality as our-America's standard. Only then will we be completely free, no longer faced with having to find what we already have.

Their-Government's Inequality

In direct opposition to this thought, special interests are regularly contributing tax-deductible portions of their already confiscated wealth to government officials in exchange for laws and regulations that provide expanded tax-sheltering benefits that encourage further wealth confiscation. From their point of view, they are simply making another investment (buying a government) that will reciprocally support Wall Street's economic interests, and thereby prevent our right of access to equity and equality.

In 2000, this nation's electoral process consumed nearly two billion dollars in campaign expenditures. The estimated 2004 political campaign expenditures — from pretentious primaries to the final anointing — may very well approach, if not exceed, three-billion dollars. When dealing with these kinds of large numbers, there is no way to determine where misfortune ends and misconduct begins. The equity of special interests can only be defeated when We, the People, have achieved an equitable human equality.

The truth is, the easier it is for the Washington Republicrats to expand their power over the now subservient majority, the more enfeebled and incompetent the citizenry becomes. At every government level, bureaucrats can easily load the dice against the common folk, whose ignorance of technicalities render them unable to defend themselves. Consider the human damage being generated throughout America by our under-funded public education system. Allowed to continue as it is, we may soon have to import enough knowledge to sustain our foreign owned corporations and the most basic of our domestic institutions.

Note: The nation's teachers can build a new seedbed of democracy in America by teaching this formula for success… Knowledge + Opportunity + Ownership = Human Dignity. By focusing on the outcome potential of our-humanity before their-profit, our children will establish a turning point that can free us all. The costs of ignorance are far more expensive than a good education.

The truth is, only democracy can provide an indestructible foundation upon which we can build an everlasting equitable human equality in all public and private activities. Any existing government rules that limit our membership in We, the People, must immediately be changed, and many such limitations now exist. America must have a constitutional doctrine of equitable equality.

English author Ivor J.C. Brown, said it best: "By equality we do not mean that everybody is alike or that every one is born into the world with a certain number of natural, inalienable rights; but simply that in the divisions of power and of happiness at which democracy aims, each must count for one, and no one for more than one, because this is the only working method. Equity is useful to remedy defects in the law or in the economic structure of society, but it must be carefully watched because it may be the tool of interested parties. On the whole it will be found that in the distribution of power the principle of equality is essential because no other method can possibly deal with large masses of people."

CHAPTER 5
REPRESENTATIVE DEMOCRACY

> *Rule by wealth,*
> *is not representative*
> *democracy.*

While we have quantified the principles of equity and equality as the only fair and balanced use of power within a democracy, we are by no means out of the woods. Rather, we are entering tangled undergrowth where we now find our representatives are working full time as their government.

With this point made clear, this nation's pretense of representative democracy, when openly intertwined with Wall Street's lack of accountability, leads to the first paradox between political equality and social equity in America. While we may believe that we have an equality of voice, the effectiveness of our sound remains at the mercy of Wall Street capitalists and their-government.

Elected to a time-measured term of office, this nation's governing Republicrats are by law immediately free to violate our individual rights until such time as an election again calls them to task. They are at liberty to promote any self-serving cause, including restrictive procedures that make their recall from elective office highly improbable and practically impossible.

Through readily available technology, a verifiable electronic voting system could provide us with a simple method of instant recall for errant politicians, which would make them far more attentive to our needs. The in-office Republicrats will, of course, never voluntarily grant this democratic right to its citizenry.

We need to try

In this first attempt to promote a real democracy in our America, there are three areas of immense concern. First, conflicting beliefs, traditions, and superstitions directly influence the public's opinion, and these powerful emotions are not easily controlled. The very act of building a legislative body that would become an accurate sounding board for the voice of the people is a task of immense complexity. Past efforts have often produced only a muddled murmur.

Second, translating the concept of responsible and accountable political representation into actual practice has historically provided special interests with the time, place, and circumstance to intentionally misdirect the people's power. There are simply too many chances for an elected representative to forget they are servants of the people. Their public expressions often come forth as "our master's voice."

Third, there arises within officialdom a never-ending audacity so typical of all who would be king. Although owing their position to the people's vote, these lofty posts create such an aura of superiority that they swiftly forget We, the People, their Ultimate Sovereign, the nation's true source of all power.

The needed solution must go far beyond obtaining fair results through a corrected election process. The damage is extensive; a salvage operation would minimize our losses, but not restore our power. Resolving the comparative value between an accurate application of the public's opinion, and the actuality of this nation's rule by the power of wealth, will not be an easy task.

The Fix is On

Gerrymandered voting districts are continually changing the rules and dividing constituencies by political party allocation. This is not done to benefit the people, but to serve the in power Republicrats. Here's one example: Pennsylvania's 19 Congressional Districts, carved out by a Republican-controlled State Legislature, elected 12 Republicans... even though Democrats held a statewide voter edge of 540,000.

Here are more examples: The Federal Electoral College has granted to itself the power to ignore the majority's choice in presidential elections. And, the U.S. Supreme Court can, and has, overridden the voting rights of We, the People.

Fourteen of the most populous states can elect and thereby control the people's House of Representatives. In direct opposition, half of the U.S. Senators, plus one, representing our smaller states with less than one-fourth of the nation's population, can control the U.S. Senate and refute the demands of the majority. Nothing remains of the constitutional representations we thought would check and balance our equal rights.

Be reminded — one-vote victories count as much as unanimous approval. When any one political party alliance wins a great many U.S. Senate seats by a small majority in twenty-six of our less populous states, while the other party wins all the rest with large majorities, the reverse of representative democracy is the end result. A majority of voters would have only a minority of representative members, and the ensuing government could legally set in motion powerful activities in direct opposition to the wishes of the people. None of this is government by any measure of Ultimate Sovereign representation. It is government by the government, and for the government.

Elections carried on under such conditions are comparable to betting, with a bookmaker we will never see again, on horses that only run in fixed races. We talk of the public's opinion, but even when most widely articulated, their-government simply doesn't have to listen.

Continuing optimistically towards democracy requires a mighty faith in a definitely blind goddess of justice. New ideas are essential to spur the nation's progress. Right now, our America desperately needs new ideas.

There is a Solution

Although it has never happened, responsible and accountable representatives, essential to achieving democracy as we have described it, will make themselves available when the people express the need. At present, our silence has allowed their-government, but our-government will happen when we demand it

Here it must be asked: How can any American be so blind as to close their eyes and voluntarily accept the rampant despotism of rule by the powers of confiscated wealth? Why are so many Americans unwilling to vote and thereby exercise their right of full participation in every election, to assure their voice will be heard? The answers completely escape me.

It appears that too many have been convinced they "can't beat City Hall." Have we forgotten? We, the People, are the foundation that supports and maintains City Hall.

Though it was not my intended purpose, I would be remiss if I did not again and again submit my concerns with practical proposals about ideas and ideals aimed toward democracy in America. To this end, my primary thrust is to continually clarify and inform my readers of the potential benefits that democracy would naturally deliver.

For the present, it is sufficient to demonstrate that before we can expect to make democracy a reality, we will have to consider the lopsided foolishness of our existing political machinery, face a significant number of distortions and lies, and then come to a conclusion.

The complexities can be simplified and the alternatives we offer may help you reach a sound and fair decision. But even under the most favorable circumstance, our collective opinion will not always be strictly accurate. Reality will always have a few rough edges. In fact, the idea of ever having absolute perfection may actually be a scary thought, for how could we make any further improvements?

Partisan Purpose

One big problem is the political party system we have. Like any disciplined and organized system, it is automatically capable of producing only self-serving benefits. When the majority of its members are passively indifferent and submissively uncritical, this pipeline of power is subject to easy abuse, from alert connivers and manipulators who stand ready to benefit.

Democracy in America will remain but a very dim light, at the end of a very long tunnel, until the American people are awakened to the impending economic disaster that is slowly but surely extinguishing our power as this nation's Ultimate Sovereign.

The truth is, a conservative plutocracy vs. a liberal plutocracy, is the only difference between America's existing political parties. Degradation by the power of confiscated wealth is obvious in both, where lobbyists are pressing the final destruction of any remaining aspects of democracy in America. And there has been literally no resistance by the public at large. Allowed to continue unchallenged, this Republicratic monstrosity will eventually destroy the genuine and valuable elements of basic political conflict, leaving nothing but a mindless and despicable humanity.

This is the confusion created by allowing Wall Street lobbyists to control America's politics, as previously shown in our discussion of equality and equity. It would be a waste of time to tarry over this now obvious error. A more pressing task is to expose any continuation of their more obvious distortions. Just keep in mind, when the fox is in charge of the hen house, survival of the chickens is always doubtful.

Despite a small but growing resentment toward this nation's predominately two party system, its justification still remains. The flow of social, economic, and political concepts run naturally into two directly opposing channels. In fact, the two-party system could never have attained such a tremendous hold on the country if it had not been consistent with our basic desire for a decisive majority process.

But legislative actions, when taken only for partisan purposes, can be infinitely dangerous, for they are capable of wielding the nation's resources and thereby, can become a merciless master of the majority they were intended to serve. How often must we be reminded that "the price of liberty is eternal vigilance"?

Every group must have leaders, every association its officials, and historically these organizations have required huge displays of wealth and power. In America, major election funds are supplied by individual capitalists and Wall Street executives and these rich men, having paid the piper, proceed to call for laws that will shield their self-serving and often illegal activities from restrictive regulations as well as taxation.

Through an endless parade of special-interest lobbyists, Wall Street easily suppresses any awkward proposals from the people while they elicit sympathetic administration from their bought-and-paid-for Republicrats. Instead of being controlled democratically from below, the government is directed and controlled from above — all at the expense of the unacknowledged, already over-burdened everyday Americans. Or, as Alexis De Tocqueville stated: "Democracy is forced to retreat before the tradesmen and capitalists."

Thus, the American voter's choice is invariably between a lesser of offered evils or distorted images — never real issues. Candidates stand by their special interest campaign contributors, but it is the people who vote them into office that will pay in the end.

To get big, we need to think small.

These plutocratic conditions, allowed to continue, will inevitably destroy the majority's ability to act or even think, at which point few will be allowed to question any shortage of goods or services for the masses. Eventually, the need for the masses themselves may be questioned. The American Dream simply cannot become a reality if our highest goal is subservient mediocrity.

How did we allow this destruction of our human rights to come about? What is the crime? Who is the criminal? Are not the Wall Street lobbyists just as destructive to our humanity as any dealer of drugs? Is their addictive high for ever-more wealth and power a lesser of evils, if in the end we lose the last of our individual rights?

As it is, we are confronted with firmly entrenched national standards of wage-slavery and taxation without representation, legally preempting the people's power. But have faith and stay alert, we have an alternative. Democracy, with its simplistic tenets and majority concerns, can provide an escape to a common ground for the people's point of view.

Every nation's power begins with the desire and interest generated in its smallest communities. Therefore, if democracy in America is to succeed, individuals must feel its need to exist at the grassroots level.

As we have said, the governing of the people must be a result of public opinion, and the final shape of the nation's opinion must be an end-result of the sum of the smallest political units — our precincts and wards. If individuals in local politics decide to make a difference, their message will rapidly filter its way to the top.

However, when large numbers of people are being dealt with, achieving fair and just representation is always an extraordinarily difficult task. An enlightened government calls for dividing power among the people, a procedure we have called representative democracy. Its first priority is to establish an election process that is fair; ensuring the winning of every elective post is neither by private fortune nor gerrymandered arrangement. Vitally important, a system of instant recall must be readily at hand to withdraw individual vote support when the elected no longer serve the majority.

Be reminded, We, the People, can win if we are willing to meet the challenge to both start and complete the building of our-America. It is a massive construction project that could take centuries, or just one election. Let those who want to continue this Republic's politics of rule-by-wealth, join or stay in the Republican Party. For the rest of us, we can take over the Democratic Party and start practicing its namesake, democracy.

It will then be left up to We, the People, to choose and elect our-representatives who will either keep what we have, a republican plutocracy, or install a more democratic form of capitalism as this nation's governing (political and economic) philosophy. Backed by the Ultimate Sovereign power of the majority, we will either build our-America and thereby lay claim to our well-earned inalienable right to "life, liberty, and the pursuit of happiness," or continue our subservient existence. The option is ours, at least for now.

CHAPTER 6
GUARANTEED DEMOCRACY

> *When Democracy overtakes boredom our-America becomes a reality.*

The truth is, we live in a Republic of States, not a Democracy of Human Beings. So, this pursuit of an alternative governing philosophy is more than a mere academic challenge. It is a "stand up and get counted" opportunity to finally possess our-America.

When We, the People, elect someone to any public office, we are authorizing him or her to use discretion and vote as seems right at the time. But they are human, and like our selves are subject to the pressures of time, place, and circumstance.

While we believe the responsibility of political office should weigh heavy upon the honesty and integrity of every elected public official, there is never any assurance they will carry out the people's mandate. It is one thing to have voted for a public servant. It is quite another to have him follow our every wish or meet any demand.

Though elected to be our representative, once in office, they are transformed as if by magic to master of all they survey. There is first the business of building a war chest to finance their next election, then there is the actual law making process, followed by, if there is time, keeping the public trust. Here, our frustration involves tracing their movements and tracking their decisions — where responsibility is improbable and accountability is impossible.

Our-Representative... or theirs?

We, the People, must never doubt that a small group of committed citizens can create change. History has shown us. It's the only thing that ever has.

To find our starting point, we must return to our roots. The real meaning of the term "representative" is what produces our confusion. As voters, we make our individual choice between candidates we actually know very little about. We decide upon a candidate on the basis of a media blitz concerning either generally vague or totally negative campaign issues.

But once elected, officials must deal with a multitude of problems. They cannot consult with the individual elector on every decision they make or every vote they record. They cannot run back and forth between constituency and legislature, and they cannot poll their electorate on every issue.

They are there for the term of office, and we are stuck with him until the next election. The best we can hope for is that they will do no serious harm, and that at least some of their behind the scene activities may eventually become known.

Ascension to powerful political office is an ego-exhilarating experience that can quickly overwhelm even the best-intentioned candidate. In the hands of an unscrupulous individual, such power is easily abused and the people's needs quickly forgotten.

Guaranteed Democracy

Have you noticed how all Republicrats avoid direct answers to even the most basic questions? For all too many of us, their electable image has become far more important than their integrity, or a plan to actually solve the nation's problems. We may be told "mission accomplished," or "bring it on," but we'll never know the truth until it's too late.

Be reminded, once elected, our representatives have an unspecified use of our sovereign power, a mandate for good, or for ill. For this reason alone we should value their personal character and individual qualifications as far more important than party loyalty or a stand upon any given issue.

While party allegiance alone may force some decisions, it is equally true that all issues will attract a variety of special interest pressures. Resisting these multi-directional forces requires resilient representatives with strong ideals and fearless independence. From a strict standpoint of the people's power, these favorable qualities can also be used against our interests, but that is the way it is with all good things.

The truth is, achieving a guaranteed democracy from our existing governing system would seem to be impossible. Without a complete change, the best we can hope for is that all Republicrats will never be totally of like mind, for that would become an even greater tyranny, beyond the comprehension of any electorate.

Here, it is interesting to note, individual and independent views by some elected officials may accidentally produce a representation of a minority point of view that might otherwise go completely underrepresented. Such honest, though rare, occurrences, are outward signs of what is possible.

The Legislature

Beyond the individual representative, we will now consider the collective legislature. Although its function should be simplicity itself, with a constant effort to pursue the common good of all the people, this is rarely, if ever, the way it is.

What guarantee can we obtain that this collective body will not usurp our granted power and use it against the will of the electorate? Historically a time limit, imposed upon the term of an elective office, has been our only protection. The thinking here is that left to legislate too long, without advice from the electorate, they will by secretive process produce a self-sustaining plutocracy, which is the truth in today's America.

It would seem some term should be established, but what term is appropriate? Is two years too short? Is six years too long? Logic and reason tell us that the shorter the term the more democratic the assembly, for time would favor the Ultimate Sovereign (the people) over the Legal Sovereign (our elected representatives). But the work of government must be done and imposition of too many checks and balances, though well intentioned, may instead have a weakening and destructive effect.

At present, the terms and requirements for any political office in America are quite varied. In the pursuit of power through political office, every campaign becomes a dilution of civic duties, every election a major dislocation of the business of government. Displacing what should be our most valuable leadership, they are forced to raise huge amounts of reelection funds and again qualify because of a passage of time, not because they have done wrong. Yet if they do wrong, they are invariably allowed to fulfill their term without recall.

Is there a good solution? Yes! In a true democracy, elected representatives would remain at their posts until recalled by a systematic withdrawal of electorate support. For every election is but another opportunity for special interests to buy another government. The election laws and process need to be carefully watched, and only purposely changed, for they are every nation's weakest point.

Be reminded, even a guaranteed democracy, once achieved, cannot transmit itself into action unless the people are willing to continuously support and maintain it, for citizens rights left unattended will quickly wither and die.

CHAPTER 7
LEGISLATIVE GOVERNMENT

> *Our tower of strength must be made of the best people available.*

The truth is, this nation's legislative government activities must somehow be taught to accept and agree with the public's opinion. This is a monumental challenge that must be met. While the government must be free from wanton attacks upon its operational system, it must, by the same token constantly protect and serve the rights of We, the People.

At this point, it is important to correctly identify the existing Congress as "The National Chamber of Commerce," the irresponsible source of this nation's deteriorating quality of life. The scope and magnitude of their disloyalty and incompetence towards our majority rights is beyond all comprehension. Their obvious denial of democratic principles, in service to special interests, should boggle the mind of every one of us.

When we, as Ultimate Sovereign, give our (vote) power to this Legal Sovereign, it is with an understanding they will do what is in our best interests. If they ignore our needs or abuse our rights, they have broken the contract, and we must immediately take corrective actions.

Suffice it to say, all that are disappointed by the political-economic system we have should take the time to study its direct effect upon their own existence and then, get out and vote. Our task is to keep describing the general principles that will lead in a positive direction towards realizing the people's power, and then map out a path that any individual can easily follow. Our continuing effort is to consistently develop the most favorable points of democracy and critique the absence of their existence in our-America.

A Gordian Knot

The truth is, the legislative functions of their-government are made purposely cumbersome and infinitely complex, even under the best of circumstances. The multiple layers of private meetings and committee activities that occur before any law receives final approval can consume an eternity. Even hurried measures with little opposition cannot avoid some form of publicity, which will invariably produce a delaying dissent from some special interest.

The question of need for a constitutional convention arises, but it must be treated in other essays, for our intent is to remain brief and yet comprehensive in this study of the merits and values of democracy. For now we must return to the main issue — the personal benefits of a real democracy, so easily achieved by merely ordering our political representatives to attend majority objectives on a day by day basis. The simplicity of this act must be forever in our mind.

Because the kind of government we have is neither what we want nor need, we must here further explore the bicameral basis of its legislative bodies. What principle underlies its choice of two competing legislatures? How does their interaction, producing more problems than solutions, interfere with our desire for democracy?

The people's House of Representatives receives its power by popular selection, from a population-counted citizenry. While the U.S. Senate, a monument to special interest control of political ego, is only a representative of each State's dominion. Is this in direct opposition to national interests? Is this territorial guardian there to purposely obstruct the Ultimate Sovereign's power? If so, why are we tolerating this deeply entrenched blockage to any possible existence of a real democracy in America?

Should the Senate be allowed to continue its checkmate capability against the nation's majority? Due to its smaller number of members, it is more easily captured by the financial leverage of special interests. They exist merely as an obstruction of the people's power, and thus, nearly always do more harm than good.

If they were to be elected on some theoretical basis of democratic equality, they would then be a direct repetition of the House of Representatives and therefore useless. As it is, the Senate is most certainly a violation of the primary democratic principle of one-man one vote, as the people have been led to believe democracy should be.

While the solution is a complex issue, the problem of an upper house is, in principle, a simple one. In a real democracy the population does not need two assemblies coming from the same electorate and exercising the same function. Believers in a true democracy will simply prefer to eliminate the Senate.

Before we pass on to the more challenging task of controlling government officials, there is reason to again put forth the concept of instant recall. An infuriated electorate must have a method of bringing errant politicians to heel. Why must we wait for two, four or six years, when an elected legislator has ignored his promised performance? The knowledge that they can easily shuffle out of trouble on any issue with merely the lapse of time, is often the very essence of their uncontrollable power. Only the stubborn logic of folded arms supported by the power of an instant recall can bring a sitting politician to use their common sense.

Special Interest Lobbyists

Direct actions by Wall Street lobbyists, at work in every office of government, directing every economic as well as social issue, are an obvious violation against the people's rights. We do not intend by this accusation to discredit all direct actions, for revolutions are also a direct action and all revolutions are not necessarily wrong. Many civil rights and liberties, which most people would acknowledge to be good, were actually won by direct action. But direct action should be a rare medicine and not a daily addiction, and revolutions should only be sought as the last resort.

Because all private campaign contributions are direct actions that can apply a stranglehold upon the political process, they must be eliminated. If the free will of the people became active and apathy were permanently stilled, it is probable that political gamesmanship and financial maneuvering would immediately and forever cease in government. If all our problems could thus be settled, it would certainly make easy the path toward the democracy we seek.

Here and now We, the People, must oppose every special interest and lobbyist activity, for they are undermining the very idea of democracy in our-America. Placing the power of law directly in the hands of any self-serving minority openly destroys any possibility of political fairness. Every private contribution and/or corporate honorarium allocated to any government official or legislator is a direct slap in the face of what we thought was supposed to be a democracy.

Only a carefully nurtured confidence can produce an acceptable agreement, between the government and We, the People, to mutually abide by just and fair rules and cooperatively play the game. If, however, there is an unacceptable breach of the rules by special interests, then direct action or even revolution may become fully justified.

Interestingly, negative results can also be obtained through direct action that turns against the people it was intended to help. Adoption of lobbyist tactics by labor unions, for example, has in fact reduced their effectiveness. When, by endorsement, unions win too much political power, corporate interests can quickly apply opposing economic action at every level of legislative activity, making it impossible to carry on a fair and effective government.

Though unions might gain some measure of political power for their organization, they can never be in a position of complete denunciation, for they become guilty of special interest distortion of the majority's rights. Labor unions, thus engaged, no longer speak for the beneficial ownership of their wealth creating members. Their justification is reduced to collecting dues and maintaining the basis of the union's existence.

However, I do see within labor unions, a potential of leadership of a new national effort towards democracy in the workplace, a Capital Homestead Act, financed through a new Federal Reserve Bank, which will fully fund Community Centered (CCSOP's) and Employee Stock Ownership Plans (ESOPs). Hopefully the unions will recognize this opportunity to promote the power of new-wealth creation by America's labor force.

Regarding every form of direct action in political affairs I feel that, if the people are really opposed to the conduct of its government, it could in some cases achieve change through the next political campaign. Or, as previously suggested, change could also occur by a system of instant representative recall — a direct action in rebuttal to any point in question.

We Need a Plan

Bringing any branch of government into an arena of public contempt will upset the community apple cart, though it may at times become our civic and moral duty to act. Only through an orderly method of open voting, backed by the power of instant recall, can our individual free will be combined to democratically decide if and when the government has broken all bounds of decency and must be fought tooth and nail.

While one voter may emphasize the necessity of maintaining the historical Constitution, even at a cost of inconvenience, another might risk any horror to correct an irresponsible political act. It is along these lines that every American will have to decide whether a crisis is indeed at hand.

Together and separately, we must carefully explore both our political beliefs and what values we should place on our citizenship, as well as our very existence. While we still have our right to vote, we will need to individually contrast and balance two perspectives; the value of liberty and justice in a true democracy, in comparison to the existing plutocracy intent on containment and subservience of We, the People.

Their government will of course vigorously oppose the very idea of democracy. They will argue that the people should not be allowed to use their Ultimate Sovereign power to force resolution of any national problems like: Their out of control National Debt. Their under funded educational, Medicare and Social Security programs. The millions of Americans now living in poverty. Or, Wall Street's ever-increasing International Trade Deficit.

Or they may correctly argue, America is a republic, and democracy does not exist. The super-rich already control both the government and the public's political machines through their special interest lobbyists. Therefore, they have every right to achieve their self-serving goals by any means including bribery. Is that okay with you? Is this what the American people really want?

It is through this maze of rule by wealth that the seekers of democracy must continually work their way, until they confront a personal decision. Should each individual do his/her utmost to defy what we might consider to be an illegal government? History has shown us many righteous revolutionaries. But, as we have already shown, revolutions are a desperate act, particularly when we have a quick and easy alternative available upon demand.

Democracy, once in place, would automatically guarantee a responsible and accountable legislative government... whose work would always be in the interests of We, the People. This sounds to me like it's the right thing to do.

CHAPTER 8
GOVERNMENT OFFICIALS

> *What will make you hunger for a democracy that eliminates poverty?*

The truth is, America's non-existent democracy was stillborn in 1776, when the power of wealth corrupted its first officials. The people, by failing to exercise their majority rights, allowed their power to pass into the hands of a plutocratic minority that, to this very day, doles out minimal gratification in return for its uncontested continuation.

Just as the never-ending audacity of elected representatives can ruin the personal liberties of democracy, appointed government officials can be even more destructive to the individual rights of all. While the elected representatives play at the business of law making, a far greater danger to the American people comes from appointed (some say anointed) government officials.

Their power is instantaneous, and the damage they do is ever lasting. In only one moment of time they can arrange an economic commitment or an undeclared war. A Cabinet level official may casually waste what an army of taxpayers will labor years to pay for. And, just as the people do not hear of these actions until the nation is committed, so none of us will hear of the costs until the final invoices come in.

According to this nation's check and balance system, a presidential appointment to a Cabinet level office is dependent upon, and accountable to, the legislature. A sound and healthy theory, since the legislature is, in turn dependent upon, and accountable to, the electorate. But, as we have shown, it never has worked like it is supposed to.

The nation's president is the connecting link between these appointed officials and the elected legislators. But of what real value is this connection when presidents, using Executive Privilege, can avoid being questioned about casual misdemeanors or even criminal behavior? Any secretive act or operational blunder that may find its way into the public arena can be easily stonewalled or met with silence and evasion, "in the interests of national security." This becomes a secret place to hide errors and provide advantages for everyone except We, the People.

Thereby, the president, who is in turn shielded by privilege, shields potentially dangerous government officials serving in strong and powerful positions. Perhaps we have stressed this sleaze-factor too much, but in light of recent events there is nothing to be gained by closing our eyes to the obvious realities being thrown in our face.

The flip side of this ever-present stalemate is bureaucrats in the government's employ, who make their work important by making our very existence nothing but troublesome. These appointed and career government officials can easily create excessive extremes in every facet of government function — a terror of opposites. They can make elaborate rules and regulations that prove beneficial only for themselves, or the current administration's self-serving economic theory, always at the expense of the public's welfare. Against any interruption of their potentially destructive disorder, there is a demand for civil service protection, a continuation of the inept and ineffective in perpetuity.

During international turmoil, this nation's foreign diplomats rarely include common sense in their displays of pompous arrogance. Protected by executive privilege, foreign policy officials are free to take secret actions that can have the most terrible and far-reaching results. With minimal regard for human life, they bargain away money, materials, and territory as play making pawns, with inconceivably far reaching and long term results.

Their claim of need for great secrecy is the very reason these diplomats should be required to constantly acknowledge that the nation's power comes only from the free will of their Ultimate Sovereign. For in the end it will be We, the People, who will count our losses in blood and get stuck with the cost as well. In return, we will be shown official disgust for our status as the nation's paymaster and a plentiful source of human cannon fodder. The nation's ship of state needs judicious steering, but why is its course always between Republicratic wants and Wall Street demands?

What can be done? Is there any possible way to effectively check on the doings of these all-powerful bureaucracies? Can we create a system of "sunshine laws," making these officials' go public in meeting their responsibility to the people? Protecting and serving, with honesty and integrity, must somehow become the national standard for America's government officials. Arrogance is not an exclusive right of politicians. These appointed officials' display it frequently, and equally as well.

The Power of Our Vote

Changing this nation's governing philosophy is going to be a tough job, one that can only be accomplished by us. For it is the ordinary, every day, hands-on, hard-working, new-wealth creating American who must carry the weight of government. When the weight becomes unbearable, we must be able to bring the whole thing down and begin anew.

The power of our vote must be a constant reminder that a determined people's majority is this nation's Ultimate Sovereign. It is a mighty weapon, more than capable, of removing forever the last vestiges of our subservient existence.

Here we need to ask ourselves: Do we really have the right to complain when less than half of the eligible Americans empowered themselves to decide the 2000 national election? On a more personal level, do we have a right to complain of crime in our streets, when the conditions we have allowed actually encourage this kind of activity as a primary path out of poverty for many of our poorly educated masses? Are we so mentally subdued and conditioned that we should continue accepting the best government that money can buy?

Our first duty to the American Dream is to wake up. Before we can extract any guarantees for what is supposed to be our-America, we must first build both the energy and the ability to do our civic duty within our own backyard.

The argument that I raise, is to insist that each American must become aware that democracy is not alive and well in America. The people's power already weakened by Wall Street greed, means every path we travel, and every effort we make toward actual democracy in America will be vigorously opposed.

Neither elected representatives nor appointed government officials now feel, nor even fear, the people's anger. Now well beyond our reach, they continuously build ever-higher monuments to their hallowed and enduring gods of greed, profit, and self.

Here and now it is time for We, the People to acknowledge and accept the burden of our individual responsibility within a true democracy. Together, we can and we must confront those who are denying our Ultimate Sovereign rights.

The question is, what will motivate us to accept our-responsibility, and demand their-accountability? Our Ultimate Sovereign vote by itself could bring democracy into being without any further action. What will challenge you enough to exercise this right?

Be reminded that our right to vote is a very different thing from our ability to make an intelligent choice. Unless and until each individual is willing to become a knowledgeable voter, we will remain, as we are, the unfettered slaves of Washington Republicrats, Wall Street's America, and their-government's officials.

A plutocratic republic such as ours, with its veneer of democracy, is perhaps, one of the most insidious forms of rule known to man. Fortunately for us, no other type of government could withstand its own contempt as much as our own. Only vigilance and hard work will correct the errors we have allowed, and for We, the People, already busy with our own greedy affairs, these are tiresome but vitally essential issues.

CHAPTER 9
DEMOCRACY AND CAPITALISM

> *Putting the nation right means keeping the wealth we create.*

Democracy is a pretty word with a pleasant sound but plutocracy is the ugly truth. This unseemly comparison deserves an explanation, and demands a careful investigation. When we allow the economics of materialism to control all of this nation's political activities, we are denying both our individual and collective responsibility and accountability for our being subservient to their government.

Thus far we have traced the meaning of the word democracy and we have explored some of the ways and means of rule by wealth. We have described the mechanics of the nation's political machinery, and cautioned alertness to government officials and political representatives who have exchanged their call to serve the people with a mandate of self-serving purpose.

We will now confront the plutocratic capitalists who leverage the non-existence of democracy as their personally convenient and thus profitable illusion. The advanced business skills developed by these practitioners of marketing, finance and accounting, (a Wall Street transliteration of lie, steal, and cheat,) now directs the nation's social, political, and economic activities in a singular perspective of materialism, profit and greed.

These capitalists will, of course, prefer that America's history not be the truth — an open and honest record of their pyramidal schemes of usurped power, wealth confiscation, and slavery in all its various forms.

Is it not yet obvious? For as long as these politically powerful capitalists can successfully control every level of government, this nation will never be allowed to perform as a democracy. Yet the promised-but-never-delivered American Dream will forever pour forth from this honey-bucket mirage, politically luring us deeper and deeper into social paralysis by economic analysis

The truth is, America's hands-on, new-wealth creating workers are still being led down endless paths of unfettered wage-slavery. Always limited by Wall Street's minimum wage standard, this nation's promise of "liberty and justice for all" means absolutely nothing if we continue to subserviently surrender our ownership of the new-wealth that we individually create.

The primary problem of, this government endorsed, inequitable equality is that it so easily excludes the majority from participation in its inalienable rights. Through a well-planned and coordinated system of limited education and controlled income levels, lower income groups are kept outside the limited opportunities that do exist for America's middle class. The middle class in turn, are just as easily kept from obtaining enough ownership to become part of the wealthy few.

Preventing our unity by endlessly dividing or defining us by a hundred and one minority issues is essential to the capitalist's success in controlling their-government and weakening our strengths. Thereby, they are completely free to manipulate the nation's economy, cleverly concealing a burgeoning national debt behind their president's declarations of national prosperity.

Washington's Republicratic guarantee of Wall Street profits will undoubtedly explain every success and justify every failure in American history, but this single perspective would be totally misleading. The preservation of our humanity must come from something greater than commercial profiteering applied by egomaniacs.

The false assumption that man is strictly an economically determined creature, bound only by his drive towards an eternal gain, is fundamentally unsound. This nation's human resources must be nurtured without the bias of inequitable economics.

If, however, we continue to accept our subservient existence, and this nation's plutocracy remains intact, any hope for political fairness, social equality, or economic justice will be lost forever. The simplicity of the solution lays in our acceptance of democratic principles. Majority rule is the real power. We can choose to be part of the solution or continue excluding ourselves so that we can continue to complain.

Or, by coming together, we can change the course we've taken; the mistakes we've made do not have to be repeated. To assure our survival, we must search for and find leaders who are capable of using imagination with discretion, and knowledge with dedication. But even this will not help unless there is first a common agreement on a priority of our-humanity before their-profit.

The Power of Confiscation

The first mark of power began by combat, the caveman's use of physical strength to enforce confiscation from the weaker members of his clan — thereby established human subservience. Therefore the mark of power we speak of is really the ability to control the actions of others. If these statements hold true, wealth itself is not the source of power, it is merely an end result of confiscation, the primary objective of corporate merchants, empire builders and war mongers who would have it all.

Perhaps a generalized definition of all wars will explain our nation's currently degrading state of foreign affairs. Some wars are strictly defensive. Many have been purposely waged for territorial or economic goals, a forced confiscation of material and property. But most have been inspired by political or religious arrogance, an imposition of one belief over another, a personal dream of empire or world domination.

All that any war can ever prove is that the common man can be conditioned to work like a slave, face great danger, and undergo self-sacrifice and extreme hardship for reasons he barely understands. The instigator's purpose may be to expand their territory, confiscate natural resources, or forcibly impose their political ideology or religious beliefs, but the guys in the trenches will never share in any of the benefits. Through militant conditioning the foot soldier will fight and die, for god or country, and the capitalists will gather all the profits.

Too obvious to be ignored, this military-industrial mentality of confiscation, legal or otherwise, combined with importing far more than we are exporting, is the Republicrats only method of achieving economic growth— and it's being paid for by our children's future.

Stop and think, We, the People, desperately need to create and keep more new wealth, not consume more imported stuff we don't really need, bought with money we don't really have. The truth is, we're spending yesterday's wealth, and not replacing it.

Here it is interesting to note that America's educational system is inadvertently enhancing the capitalist's lust for ever-more wealth. The affluent and more capable students are not taught the values of human relationships, moral vitality, or the how and why of wealth creation. Instead, the brightest and best are channeled into business administration and law, the two best training grounds for wealth confiscation.

The students that fall through the cracks of this system are left without sufficient knowledge to fully access opportunity and fairly acquire ownership, the legitimate pathways to human dignity. Is it any wonder that many of them end up qualified only for dead end jobs, living in poverty, getting lost in the welfare system, or turn to criminal behavior as their only access to the power of wealth? Perhaps this is why this nation's prison population is over two million, and growing.

One more badly defined objective, put in place by one more self-righteous republicrat, can easily cause more thousands of unwilling martyrs. Today's result is a completely wrong-headed international arrogance that has led too many Americans to fight and die. It is thus that many empires have come and gone. Is America next?

Step Back and Think

When we build an over whelming military might of "shock and awe," and combine it with one man's certainty that he is always right, the temptation to impose his political or religious beliefs at gun point is a guarantee that both sides will lose their sons and daughters. Running these wars on tax cuts for the rich and borrowed money, a free falling dollar is now guaranteeing an unavoidable decline in our overall standard of living.

It is through this kind of mindless national purpose that we are somehow being convinced that (as unfettered wage slaves) we must have masters. Should we in honest consciousness accept this as the final destiny for We, the People?

Note: The economics of plutocratic capitalism have even overwhelmed the economics of socialism, by simply wearing it down and then absorbing it. Still, there are individuals who will pursue their equally misdirected socialistic goals, trying to weave their core ideas into the texture of society.

The truth is, if politically approved confiscation is the actual source of power, then all existing governments rule by the power of confiscation. Thus, changing the economics of a nation, without changing its overall governing policies, would be little more than an exercise in a different form of frustration. The reality of an entire world held in check by profit before humanity has distorted the whole concept of "liberty and justice for all". But have faith, democracy in America will happen.

Here it is interesting to add that early religions tried in vain to pit their versions of morality against the power of wealth. But the ruling heads of state quickly controlled the religious by teaching them how to accumulate wealth and property from their followers, leading many religions to become the wealth absorbing institutions they are today. While there is no reason to concern my readers about the influence of democracy upon religion, the opposite is great cause for alarm. For even those who detest all religious institutions draw some inspiration from their teaching. Yet, only our natural morality should set governing policies in our-America, and there must be a clear separation of church and state

In our never-ending search for the true source of all power, we must constantly ask: What idea will finally entice humanity to seek its own perfection? And the readily available answer is democracy, with its commitment to an equitable human equality, an actual delivery of "liberty and justice for all."

While profit and greed have carried a few self-serving men to triumph over all they survey, only ideals of common concern can give humankind the inspiration needed to ultimately achieve an enduring victory. Only by using our free will, with a singular focus on an equitable human equality, can we set ourselves free our inherited bondage. And only We, the People, are qualified to set our own standards, and then govern through the principles that would flow naturally within a democracy.

Wealth as Power

Another quick look back at American history will demonstrate the futility and folly of this nation's moral, economic, and political distortions. Be reminded, America's founding fathers were landed gentry, and most of them deplored the possibility of Ultimate Sovereign control. Therefore, they chose to establish a National Senate of state representatives to guard against the nation's majority power in the people's House of Representatives.

Ultimately, their successors have methodically controlled the masses by limiting and thus controlling public education. As a result, a corporate controlled media is now force-feeding a socially conditioned, half-educated nation with carefully censured information. Interestingly, corporate media power is also used to purposely misinform and influence government officials, which can be even more dangerous than Wall Street's control of the legislative and executive branches of government.

Is it not time to admit that every public claim to democracy has been little more than a complete farce? When a politically enforced three-tiered class system has successfully stymied an equitable distribution of national power, where, if at all, has the Ultimate Sovereign right of the people made any difference?

The truth is, their-government administration is carried on by secret conferences between Wall Street and Washington, where rules and regulations are resolved to the detriment of the 35 million Americans, locked in poverty, across the tracks from 255 million middle-class unfettered drones who perform as wage-slaves.

Occasionally, We, the people, are given a few sedatives to recondition our apathy and prolong our subservient existence. While we are not allowed to physically participate, we are allowed to pay taxes for the privilege of witnessing, from afar, the lifestyles of the rich and famous, as they partake, over and over again, in the pleasures of spending the people's wealth. Are there solutions and a course of corrective action readily available? The answer is, yes!

What will really terrify Wall Street capitalists and Washington Republicrats is a threat of equitable economics, an equality of power distribution based upon an honest accountability of the equity-ownership produced by every new-wealth creating effort. A nation wide system of Community Centered and Employee Stock Ownership Plans, completely replacing wage-slavery with the dignity of equity ownership, is the nightmare that will awaken every politician and corporate executive.

By creating both community and workplace ownership, these CCSOP's and ESOP's will equitably accommodate the economic needs of life. And once we are free, we must never again limit our overall view of human freedom to a materialistic yardstick. There are far more important things to life than commerce and industry. It is only for our individual rights, our arts and leisure, our traditions and affections that any societal guidelines from government should even exist. Deliverance of this more equitable form of human equality, combined with a fully educated populace, might even scare them straight, though I doubt it.

Wall Street has always known that subservient physical labor is the absolute essential in the maintenance and expansion of their confiscated possessions, and that withdrawal of wage-slave labor would totally undermine the power of confiscation that has allowed them to control the people. This is a main reason they are now manipulating the rules and allowing an illegal immigration, a throng of low priced servants for their garden of Eden. They have long known their downfall will come when the American workforce begins to fully realize that special interest control of the government is being used to pre-empt the individual's right to own the new-wealth created by We, the People.

We Have Alternatives

Simply stated, the nation's greatest honors should be accorded to the creators of new-wealth, not to those who specialize in wealth confiscation. Consider the paralyzing effect upon the nation if the hands-on, every day American wage-slaves simply decided to not share their productivity with those who only survive by living off the sweat of others.

Aside from the hands-on workers' own immediate families, entire communities would perish. The self-serving financial hucksters of Wall Street and all of their cohorts, and sub-cohorts on down the line, might at best survive only a month or two before their inevitable collapse. Their-government might initially be in place, but Wall Street's power of confiscation (that has kept these Republicrats in office) would now be gone.

Only the hands-on creators of new wealth are economically indispensable, and thereby, We, the People, are the only true source of power. This is what makes democracy in our-America possible, an unfaltering foundation upon which new towers of an equitable human equality can be constructed.

What challenge would justify so abrupt an action? The creative artists of economics, with their penchant for constantly producing new versions of the emperor's invisible clothes, stand their ground mouthing phraseology that not even they understand. Yet it is the American people that have allowed this capitalistic magic folderol to continue. The nation's government openly yielding to Wall Street's special interests, shutting down factory upon factory and industry upon industry.

To this they have now added, the outsourcing of job upon job. This final crack in the plutocrat's overall scheme is providing America's middle-class with a first look at this spiral of descending economic disparity. Where, with the combined incomes of both parents, maintaining a decent quality of life is fast becoming a very real burden. The costs of a college education are already beyond the financial capabilities of many determined and dedicated parents.

To date this rapidly increasing degradation is somehow being magically concealed from the majority, who are too embarrassed or ashamed to show public concern for their private feelings. Wall Street's power now precedes any effective use of the people's waning political influence. Should we leave this as it stands? Should it be changed?

Call it what you will. When we are not individually free to pursue an equitable human equality, we are a slave to both political and economic forces. Here, as in nearly all questions of social status, the responsibility comes back to our own efforts. Because we as individuals have not shown eternal vigilance, their government no longer acts in our behalf.

Yet, if we simply accept our individual responsibility for the way it is, and we demand accountability from our political representatives, only then will we be properly exercising our Ultimate Sovereignty. That's what democracy is all about.

But suppose some property and old wealth remain in the hands of a few? Would these plutocrats still be able to dictate their rules? Given the overall intellect of the American voters, the answer would be no, because our Ultimate Sovereign power would naturally restore our-America's prime values.

Be reminded, rule by the power of wealth has only succeeded in controlling the nation by media-conditioning us to believe that what we individually say or do will not really make a difference. It is due to this self-blinding civic ignorance that the economic power of special interests has achieved the strong position that it has.

Enron, World Com, etc. — how many more Wall Street rip-offs are you willing to ignore and pay for? The truth is, the pot of gold at the end of their rainbow was stolen from our backyard.

When we do not resist the politics of special interests, we are actually approving their control of every elective office and government official. We are granting to their government a legal license to misuse taxes that only the wealth-creating workforce can generate, and thereby we remain unfettered subservient wage-slaves. The only power we have is our right to vote, and it is my hope we will eventually find the strength to save our America.

Here and Now

It will only be through an equitable use of our nation's natural resources, and its hands-on workforce creation of new wealth, that our America can be restored. At present, Wall Street holds a politically granted right to take their-profit before caring for our-humanity and this has completely undermined our nation's values. This must be changed!

E. F. Schumacher in his book titled "Small is Beautiful" said: "What is the meaning of democracy, freedom, human dignity, standard of living, self-realization, fulfillment? Is it a matter of goods, or a matter of people? Of course it is a matter of people. But people can be themselves only in small comprehensible groups. Therefore we must learn to think in terms of an articulated structure that can cope with a multiplicity of small-scale units. If economic thinking cannot grasp this it is useless. If it cannot go beyond its vast abstractions, the national income, the rate of growth, capital/output ratio, input/output analysis, labor mobility, capital accumulation; if it cannot get beyond all this and make contact with the human realities of poverty, frustration, alienation, despair, breakdown, crime, escapism, stress, congestion, ugliness and spiritual death, then let's scrap economics and start afresh. Indeed, are there not enough signs of the times to indicate that a new start is needed?"

Thus, plutocracy prevails and democracy is but an empty word. To reverse this priority, the final use of our-America's power must ultimately lie with its people, not with its corporations or its political institutions. At present the power of their confiscated wealth is strong, and the people are weak. The fault lies within us, as does the remedy.

The truth is, capitalism, a good servant, has had a bad master, it can only be put in its proper place when the people decide to favor our humanity as this nation's first priority. For this reason alone it is right to value our political alternatives completely separately from any factor of economic influence.

Are we up to the task? Are we willing to defiantly reject and replace the plutocracy we have, with the democracy we need? Only one can be in charge. The only option we have is their-profit, or our-humanity? Which will you choose?

CHAPTER 10
DEMOCRACY AND LIBERTY

> *Liberty flows naturally, but only from democracy.*

It stands to the discredit of our founding fathers that in the end, they fell under the spell of rule by wealth. Thereby they steered America towards its present condition, a Republic that is not a democracy, where "liberty and justice for all" is merely a catch phrase.

All people that hunger for liberty realize democracy is the only governing system capable of delivering this primary element of human happiness. Thus, there is just cause for these two words to continue as inseparable companions.

Dictionaries define liberty as the state of being free. Doing his own thing might be the man on the street's feeling of liberty, while the articulate philosopher would find the power of self-direction more to his liking. Many believe that liberty is simply a natural synergy of permission and authorization. It can never be obtained without effort, it can only be maintained by constant vigilance, and it is never appreciated until it is lost.

Liberty is nonexistent when Republicratic promises are not kept; when their oppressive hand lies heavily upon us; when blind allegiance without thought or question is demanded. By allowing these political hypocrites to get their way, we are too often lulled to sleep with false images of national prosperity, that is only feeding an ever-growing national debt. Is the inevitable fall of the American Empire next?

Live Free or Die

While Washington Republicrats have conditioned us to believe we are free, the freedom we have is not equal. The truth is, when we allow ourselves to be intimidated into any form of subservience, we are not free to determine for ourselves the ways and means by which we will live.

From this it must be said: our right to liberty must never be taken for granted. If it does not make everyone free, no one is free. This point may seem obvious, yet current events suggest this may not be understood, for this nation's managers have long ignored the millions of Americans living in poverty, and the multi-millions more that are just barely getting by. But they must listen soon, for when the cries stop, direct action will begin and the nation will grind to a halt.

Now ruled by a self-anointing upper class that imposes their will upon the people, we are somehow convinced that everything is being done in the nation's best interests. But the "best" they speak of doesn't include We, the People.

The proof is found in their-America's rapidly declining world influence, which is being driven ever downward by a war-mongering greed. We now find our homeland defense forces ordered (without just cause or national purpose) to invade, occupy, or fight for our best export, some other nation's democracy, freedom or liberty. These claims display a self-righteous dictatorial arrogance, a common trait among world power bullies, self-serving governments, and all empires destined for failure.

As was previously shown, our quality of life is easily diminished whenever the majority becomes indifferent to the nation's direction. A resulting oligarchy (government by a few) takes over, and the majority allows itself to be driven by an irresponsible authority, at which point our individual liberty is steadily reduced, and then finally lost. The loss of our individual liberty affirms the loss of democracy. So the question now becomes: Will democracy save our America and assure liberty, as we understand it?

From every minority's point of view, majority rule is frequently declared the most insidious form of tyranny. Yet individuals banding together, as an enlightened majority, would be a far better safeguard for minority rights than America's existing plutocracy. The common sense of this is reason enough to also realize no minority that rules by the power of confiscated wealth will ever allow individual liberty.

If we are now willing to accept the direct relationship between liberty and democracy, we must also commit ourselves to a more detailed inquiry into the connection between our individual self and our Legal Sovereigns. Keep in mind, the common goals of We, the People, must always be stronger than our momentary differences.

Whenever and wherever we unite in common action, our need for individual liberty always exists. Within this scope there is also a need to assure that each individual's right to human dignity will never be violated by commercial mandate or government rule.

Consider this: when we only have men of authority providing authority, they will forever deliver nothing but rules and regulations of containment and limitation. For example, Wall Street lawyers and accountants wrote our present 15,000 page income tax laws. By design, the law's complexity confuses the man in the street, methodically draining wealth from the creative, product-producing workforce and directing it to the benefit of non wealth producing capitalists and their entire financial services industry.

Here, the terror of opposites comes into play. While most of us are capable of accomplishing almost anything, we are rarely well enough informed to know what it is that must be done. How can the people even say they have liberty, if we cannot first understand that political leadership of our-America must be completely separated from the financial manipulators of the marketplace?

The truth is, democracy in America will only happen when America's middle-class drones learn to free themselves from their unfettered wage slavery. Then they must teach those who have no hope, the have-nothing poor and all lower class wage slaves, so they too can learn how to survive and become self-sustaining members of our-America. Only then will we be able to proclaim, "No American Left Behind."

Getting Involved

The need to test this nation's character has never been more obvious. Far more important than "get mine first," our priority on the primordial elements of human dignity, (knowledge, opportunity and ownership) require an unlimited national commitment, a dedicated energy from every one of us. Only when our individual strengths unite as the majority, can swift and caring decisions be turned into everyday reality.

To accomplish our overall objectives, we must concern ourselves with two facets of our personal lifestyle: how our actions can affect our individual selves and what effect our actions will have on others.

What one may do within the privacy of one's own existence, others have no right to interfere with. Only when an individual activity has a direct effect on another citizen, or the community at large, does society as a whole have a right to become involved.

The practical issue is that most of our actions have little effect on other people, but some of our personal choices can have a wide significance. For instance, it does not matter what your taste in music is, you should not pollute my ear space by turning up the volume on your boom-box so loud that my personal liberty is violated. I will no longer be able to read, write, or think, and I will feel increasing resentment until finally, I am incapable of anything except hatred.

On a more national frame of reference, while our objective must always be as much individual freedom as is humanly possible, under certain conditions a measured interference can be justified if it serves to remove even greater barriers to our individual liberty.

For instance, compulsory education is indeed an invasion of our individual rights. But it can be defended on the grounds that it does, in the end, deliver more freedom than it destroys. Children denied knowledge, and thereby full development of their individual skills, are obviously at the mercy of their superiors in the wealth of wisdom. Only by removing a child's individual liberty, through compulsory education, do we enable them to become freethinking adults.

When any force or demand is used to violate our right to become the best that we can be, it always does great harm. This point alone should clearly establish that under no circumstance should government have or be able to use any form of restrictive economics to limit education. Rather, it must instead be obligated to provide free access to a full spectrum of knowledge, so every citizen has free access to opportunity and ownership, the core values of human dignity.

Only when we are fully informed can we clearly understand the importance of achieving and then maintaining both liberty and democracy. Here, it must be said — We, the People, are perfectly willing to sacrifice some personal liberties when we know our sacrifices will not be made null and void by official incompetence.

The Law

While continuing to be a nation of laws, the laws provided must favor our-humanity before their-profit. The truth is, however, too many laws can create more problems than solutions. The more laws there are, the tougher it is for us to remember them, and the tougher it is for the officials to enforce them. Hard to enforce legislation is individually destructive when by its excess it creates a general neglect and distrust of the law, and by its enforcement it often creates a contempt for even necessary authority.

This nation's history is loaded with the residue of laws that were enacted with great moral enthusiasm and later proven counterproductive by an impossibility of application or enforcement. Prohibition, the legal ban on the manufacture and sale of alcoholic beverages, is an excellent well-known example. It spawned a violent, uncontrollable, and destructive criminal industry that still affects our lives today. A truly wise government will maximize respect for a minimum of law.

Current counterproductive laws, such as cost-plus government contracts and Wall Street bailouts, defy any form of human logic. Must private greed always be fulfilled at the expense of the public purse?

A major question should be asked about every piece of government legislation. Can the law's objective, presumably positive, be achieved without displacing an equal or an even greater amount of good? Enforcement of excessive or often unnecessary law simply creates another commanding authority, and thereby further reduces the individual citizen to the level of a child.

This penchant for excessive law is a continuing reinforcement of mass human subservience, imposing an inequitable materialistic morality purposely designed to eliminate personal liberty. Again I say, our often-stated national purpose was to be the land of the free and home of the brave, not the land of greed and a home for the depraved. Fortunately, the public's acceptance of this distorted national purpose is beginning to wear thin.

The current foreign policy disasters, *i.e.*, the Bush/Cheney wars, may be the final proof of America's descending self-respect. Despite the multiple blunders of these preemptive invasions and occupations, Washington Republicrats continue to purposely mislead us and then rely on our passive-submissive attitude to keep us loyal and patriotic.

This kind of apathetic blind patriotism, inevitably to be followed by an unspoken disgust, is a debilitating combination that threatens the success of every generation. Smoldering with the slow fire of cynicism, it will ultimately destroy the spontaneity and imagination of the more active members of our society. Any government that even claims to be a democracy should most carefully heed this warning, for its major error is its own smug and grin of self-satisfaction.

Liberty cannot be established without morality, and morality cannot be sustained without faith. But morality like religious doctrine must never be imposed; it must come from within. Thus it is that the more that virtue is forced upon us, the more irresponsible and immature we will become. A close examination will disclose that great spiritual damage is done when overly passionate control exceeds the practical advantages that morality originally aimed for.

Any and every attempt to suppress or regulate our human thought process will in the end prove to be little more than an idle form of folly. Even if it was desirable, no force on earth can drive an individual to agree with you, though it may convince him to say falsely that he does. Nothing can control this process of free thought, for like free speech it must be left as an untouched and unhampered right. The result of any limitation placed on our freedom of speech would be the creation of compulsory liars, scarcely a positive virtue in any society.

What is Possible

It is hard to conceive any harm that can come to a fully liberated society that has freedom of thought, speech, and morality. If governing policies cannot withstand the criticisms and insults from its constituents, it must indeed be a flimsy power.

When any public activity is just, the complaints from a minority will do no harm. If they are unjust, then the critics deserve praise and full acknowledgement for their efforts on the nation's behalf.

For example, efforts to persecute those whom openly disputed and demonstrated against the still questionable national purpose of the Vietnam War were, in fact, affirming a low level of confidence that many politicians and government officials secretly shared. More recently, public and private resentment regarding the Bush/Cheney wars comes to mind.

Beyond government restrictions on our individuality, we must openly oppose interference by any of the vast numbers of religions. Of all forms of control this can be the most dangerous, an endless confrontation that would produce a tyranny of competing beliefs, far harsher than even the tyranny of all unjust laws. It is most clearly seen in the more militant cult-like religions, where the destruction of each individual's unique qualities is a primary objective.

History has recorded a horrendous number of lives lost for religious reasons, the current crusades in Afghanistan and Iraq not withstanding. There can be no fragment of value in faith adopted under any form of compulsion.

Religious beliefs are, and must remain an essentially individual feeling, a passionate aspiration combined with a conviction. Any effort to control or discipline them from without, is to deaden it within. Our belief, or non-belief, is one thing that an open society should refuse to touch, yet dictatorially demanding religionists abound.

The core values embodied in the phrase "We, the People," rests entirely on the principle that the majority will respect and protect the rights of the minorities, and in turn each minority will accept decisions that go against its will.

From this, it must be said, our focus on the principles of personal liberty must also be on the values of our humanity. Each must be allowed to stand or fall on its own merit. Any government attempt, formal or otherwise, at moral or societal control of the arts, for instance, would become a calamity when translated into law — an assigned bureaucracy clothing Venus deMilo in red tape, scarcely an appropriate attire on a goddess.

At this point, our pursuit of liberty must conclude, no one can ever prove their opponent is finally or even fundamentally wrong. All that open disagreement can accomplish is to reveal the views of both and bring them at the very least to an understanding of their differences, if not to an agreement to continue talking.

These kinds of uncertainties should not in any way discourage us from our continued pursuit of freedom of thought, speech and behavior, the self-guiding principles of our free will. Though even these principles cannot promise perfect solutions to individual problems, they will at least keep us thinking along sound and logical lines.

The truth is, an unquestioned tolerance of our individuality is a vital and primary virtue in any democracy, without it we cannot collectively survive. We truly need to guard well the rights of the cranks, the dreamers, the despised and rejected individualists, for they are preventing society from sinking into abject stagnation. Some may indeed be worthless, but others are the prophets and saviors of future generations. Destroy, ridicule and sneer at these imaginative minds and even more of our freedoms will be lost.

What We Can Do

There is little to be gained by the recall of one pompous politician if we immediately elect another just like him. Truly the first act of those that would desire to be free under the law must be, if I may paraphrase Shakespeare "to hang all the Republicrats."

The problem of Republicrats (many of whom are lawyers) comes not from their knowledge, but from the intent of their training. The information they derive from their insider activities ensure them a separate rank in society that constitutes a sort of privileged body within the intellectuals. This superiority of attitude is due to highly developed skills as master arbitrators, an isolated not very generally known skill in manipulative word games. This ability to speak a thousand words, and literally say nothing, confuses the parties in litigation and delivers little more than contempt for the truth

This insider trait is replicated throughout the nation's plutocracy, sharing the same tastes, habits and common interests. They subscribe to similar doctrines of order and formality, bear the same repugnance for any action that would lead to liberty of the masses, and have nothing but secret contempt for any government that would serve the majority.

Democracy in itself, is not a guarantee of personal liberty. It means nothing more than an equitable division of sovereign power among the people, the vital point being the way in which all power is used. It will only be correctly used when democracy is not an end in itself but merely a means to the good life that must be lived not only by a majority, but also by all members of society.

Yet, if we are asked what we hold to be a primary ingredient of democracy and the good life, we should in unison reply that its most essential element is liberty, the freedom of every individual.

CHAPTER 11

DEMOCRACY AND POWER

> *We, the People, can turn this Republic into a Democracy.*

America used the 18th and 19th century to explore, expand, prepare and define itself for its role as a world super power. Unfortunately, the 20th century was used by Wall Street to distort and expand artistically creative economics — a politically legalized confiscation of the new-wealth created by hands-on, hard working Americans. Now the question is, will the 21st century finally free us from our unfettered wage slavery?

As every-day Americans, we have been at the leading edge of every great happening on this earth and beyond in outer space. Driven by American ingenuity, this nation's vast natural and human resources have fueled an international technological explosion, an entrepreneurial energy that has literally dominated this world and placed a man on the moon.

But something keeps going wrong. The overall benefits of our achievements that should have made life in America good for all of its citizens are instead ravaging our rights of equality, shattering our natural morality and weakening our national unity.

The truth is, our heritage to future generations must include a confession of our inability to capture or even contain this plutocratic monstrosity turned loose by our forefathers. The inequities of their-government's absolute rule by the power of confiscated wealth are now splitting our nation apart.

On one side are two million millionaire capitalists displaying great wealth, privilege, and luxury. On the other side are thirty-five million Americans living in poverty and ignorance. And in between are 255 million middle-class subservient wage-slave drones that have closed their eyes to the truth and reality of our now failing empire.

In fact, the entire world must become aware of the job that we must do — a social, economic and political reconstruction of almost limitless proportions. While the wealthy few are demanding even more direct control of humankind by government force, the solution is exactly the opposite. Our humanity must be set free.

And when we are free, our creation of new-wealth must be democratically dispersed, for only then can there be an equitable human equality throughout the nation.

America is today what it has always been — an unlimited opportunity, still searching for the right time to begin. The challenge we face is to find a solution that will create harmony between opposites, a government that will lead, where We, the People, need to go.

A Quality of Life

To become a democracy, the way a democracy ought to be, we need to establish a baseline quality of life for every American. To do this we must retrieve our free will, value the common good, and accept our individual responsibility for changing what we have become — lifeless cogs within an enormous and merciless incorporate machine.

Be reminded, it is because we allowed their special interest lobbyists to reduce our political power to the most trifling dimension that Wall Street has now taken absolute control of this nation's government. However, no matter how economically clever these capitalists may become, they cannot forever balance their demands for greater profits against the myriad of Washington's undelivered Republicratic promises. We, the People, must face our ignorance of this reality, or we will soon have to accept the final destruction of our individuality.

Working together, we need to confront their-government, for this Republicratic plutocracy is keeping us in wage-slave servitude. In fact, every public activity must include a call for political and economic alternatives that will reclaim our-America and unite its people. We can and we must revitalize our individual freedom, revalue our human dignity, and restore our national unity.

The first step is to confront our own apathy. Then we must get over it, for we are self-debilitating our own existence. Granted, when a citizen is but one individual in a city of thousands and a nation of millions, it is at best difficult to believe we can make a real difference. But the truth is, even a small group of the people can play a big part in achieving any commonly set goal.

Talk to your friends and neighbors tell them the good news: democracy in America will happen when We, the People, demand it. Together, we can and we must take back our Ultimate Sovereign power and create change or we will remain as we are, enslaved to the power of the wealth that we are creating, that they are legally confiscating from us.

Think about it. Compare the size of your individual campaign contribution to the millions given by Wall Street capitalists. Your whisper, barely heard, is silenced by the size of their roar. Now ask yourself, who are the Republicrats listening to?

At present, our acceptance of the way it has always been has given Wall Street a free pass to continually expand its powers of confiscation. Trading not as patriotic American corporations but as international conglomerations, their One-World economy has overwhelmed us with a massive recovery of their-profits, and an ever-threatening expansion of our subservience. To deal with such a loose and variable connection demands a public admission of collusion between Wall Street and Washington that neither will ever admit.

The challenge is immense, for we must somehow remove and replace a collection of bloated and often meaningless government institutions that are totally controlling our subservient existence. With neither defined objectives nor limited purpose, they are now so over-burdened that they are incapable of controlling themselves. Perpetuating their own existence is their only priority.

Further, the number of former politicians and government officials who now call upon their in-power cronies, as special interest lobbyists, hired-gun insiders and agents of foreign powers, are an abomination of the supposed ethics and integrity in American government.

This legalized confiscation, that is today's plutocratic capitalism, came into prominence just after the American Civil War, when Lincoln's Homestead Act opened the west and handed the keys to the steel and railroad robber barons. Gradually widening its grasp and gathering speed, this political alliance with corporate conglomerations really accelerated during the Roosevelt years. The profiteering opportunities created by the material demands for World War II, Korea, Vietnam and our more recent string of international invasions and occupations have progressively contributed to the full flowering of today's plutocracy.

These Wall Street profiteers no longer make even a feeble attempt to conceal their control of America's quasi-representative government. They have assumed the power to make the law, then watch over and discipline its execution. They openly purchase authority over elected and appointed government officials, instructing them how to carry out their secretive economic schemes. This recession of the people's power has established an acceptance of plutocracy that, allowed to continue, may soon demand knee-bending, ring-kissing genuflection.

Carried on in backroom bargains between Washington Republicrats and special interest lobbyists, there is an intolerable misuse of public funds, lavish distributions to corporate profiteers of the people's taxes, and a general doling out of irresponsible power to those who always profit from the misfortunes of their fellow man. The end result is waste, chaos and cronyism, constant demands for increasing sacrifices by us, the every-day Americans, the hands-on creators of new-wealth.

Corrective actions are needed, authority and power must be parceled out, but what plan should be followed? Common sense provides the best answer. A well-structured system of layer upon layer of voluntary associations can best construct the proper foundation of a world-class democracy.

We can do it... You can help.

From our local City Hall to the Nation's Capitol, there is a serious political deficiency in solving the very social and economic problems these Republicrats are continually creating. Since they have proven themselves incapable of handling any more, we must find a way to reduce their workload. Some of this out-of-control power needs to be recalled and distributed back to the people. The best method of mastering these complex problems is one that allows form to follow function.

We need to focus on our individual strengths; the many sides of our natural skills and physical abilities; our individual interests in where we live and work; our leisure interests in playing or watching sports; our charitable interests in the welfare and well being of others, and our specialized interests in a myriad of consumer product activities.

In support of these varied interests, people voluntarily develop associations to advance and promote their respective personal causes. Neighbors participate in small community and educational affairs; workers may belong to trade unions or professional organizations; consumers and those involved in sports frequently form their own clubs.

A huge number of these associations are built upon brand loyalty and energy, yet rarely have they sought or accepted any civic responsibility. The potential of all this good energy, readily available from neighbor, friend, and foe, must now be socially gathered to politically correct and then build our-America.

However, when, through necessity, our first priority is to house and feed our family, any wealth controlling organization can, by threat or promise, easily overpower our struggling-to-survive individual human element. Thus, we are forced to spend more of our time and energy on keeping our job than questioning who, or what, is running the country.

The truth is, this nation's current governing philosophy can, by threat of government force, prevail over all wage-slaves, who must work every day to simply keep up their monthly payments to incorporate America. Our access to the American dream is purposely limited, and the poorer we become, the more easily we will be oppressed. Neither the have-nothing poor nor this nation's middle-class drones can ever escape from this descending spiral of cause and consequence, this human race to the bottom of the barrel.

This lack of attention to politics, when combined with our blind acceptance of incorporate subservience, now stifles any awareness of possible benefits that would naturally flow from democracy, a delivered social reality of both economic and political freedom.

The first roadblock that must be removed is Wall Street's control of government. There has always been something inhumane about the wealth confiscating operations of the industrial age, with its trend setting high salaried managers on top and low paid wage-slavery below. The inequity of worker submissiveness to a threat of willful termination continues today, even though it is widely known and accepted that a truly cooperative atmosphere would substantially improve workforce efficiency and increase productivity.

This long-standing inequity can be easily changed by demanding community ownership of all local utility and service industries, combined with employee ownership in the manufacturing of new-wealth workplace. We can then gradually expand this concept throughout the nation.

There will of course be an intense corporate resistance to the establishment of this equitable social and economic justice. But it will be easy to overcome this plutocratic minority if we commit ourselves to the common good of all the people. Please keep in mind, when there are no slaves, we will no longer need masters.

Since an equitable ownership would naturally increase our common benefits in the workplace, why should it not also be desirable to simultaneously increase individual involvement within community politics and then progressively on a national scale? A complete cooperation in working and living conditions, providing a responsible and accountable performance as determined by peers, would achieve balanced objectives to serve everyone. This is a demonstration of functional power distribution at its best. I cannot, of course, deal with so complex an issue in one paragraph but it would be irresponsible if I did not at least convey this line of purely logical thought.

What makes community and workplace ownership so vitally important is that marketplace competition in America is dying out. Most of our nation's largest industries are now owned by managed pension trusts, foreign investors, and highly leveraged financial institutions. While there is no public acknowledgement, it should be obvious that secret understandings do exist between Washington and Wall Street.

Further, it is naive to even think that market competition means anything outside the very small business arena, which is now being subdued and eliminated by our acceptance of a big box Wal-Mart mentality.

This ever-increasing global trend toward international conglomerates and highly manipulative financial cartels will only serve to further stiffen rule by the power of wealth. In short, America is being consumed by its own creation, greed.

If, however, you prefer watching mind-conditioning television instead of voting to stop unfettered slavery, the task is hopeless and the battle already lost. But the challenges and risks are worthwhile, and the struggle will indeed be a glorious and noble one.

The success or failure of this nation must not be left to Wall Street capitalists and Washington Republicrats. It must instead, be decided by We, the People, working together, to evolve this Republic of States into a Democracy of Human Beings.

We need to try.

There has always been something morally wrong about a national system that legislatively endorses and then tax shelters the confiscation of wealth without exertion. The destructive hand of absentee ownership grabs at everything and gives nothing in return. We have seen this and every appearance must be exposed.

Together, we need to conduct a first experiment in democracy. We need to find out if We, the People, can actually win political freedom by exercising our Ultimate Sovereignty. Only by fully and fairly democratizing our America, through a combined development of community and workplace ownership, can we find our way. The alternative is to merely continue as subservient wage-slaves under Wall Street's control.

To begin the building of our-America, the community at large will have to organize itself as a trading body and take over the means of production and distribution. All productivity and services would then become cooperative by employee ownership. The question is, how would it to be administered?

With community and workplace ownership as our first priority, interference from non-participants must be totally unacceptable. With equitable ownership within each given industry, the necessary leadership would naturally emerge by a self-selection among employees within that industry, not from externally appointed management. There is no hope for democracy in our nation if we cannot also establish democratic principles in the workplace and within the communities in which we live.

Please note: while democracy in the workplace will provide equity ownership, it will not guarantee higher wages or security by tenure. Our individual possession of human dignity would be the principle benefit from such an equitable distribution of wealth and power. Every worker in trade or craft would be a human being and not a tool; a workman and not a machine; a self-governing wealth creating individual and not a wage-slave; a responsible participant in effort and equity; and not the implement of an unseen master.

Be reminded, just as we have shown that plutocratic capitalism is not the solution for people's needs, neither is national socialism, for it creates a gigantic political machine that grinds its own citizens to a pulp. The current effort to implement capitalistic principles into the Russian and Chinese economies affirms the inevitable failure of political as well as economic socialism.

Regardless of the method, playing fast and loose with the management of numbers will never be the solution. We, the People, must insist on absolute respect for each individual's human dignity, and this will find its natural expression in shared power through employee ownership of every enterprise.

Here are several public comments made by Ronald Reagan during his last term in office: "Could there be a better answer to the blindness of Karl Marx than millions of workers individually sharing in the ownership of the means of production? That debt payments can be reduced, government businesses privatized and made more efficient, and employee ownership expanded, all as part of a mutually reinforcing plan is an exciting idea."

He then added as an afterthought: "I can't help but believe that in the future we'll see in the United States and throughout the Western world, an increasing trend toward the next logical step, employee ownership. It's a path that benefits a free people."

The sad part of these statements is that Reagan was referring to his administration's efforts to bail out private interest bank loans in Central and South America. Yes, the Republicrats are obviously aware of the American dream that workplace democracy could deliver. But the question is how can We, the People, get our share of this dream?

CHAPTER 12
DEMOCRACY AND OPPORTUNITY

> *We have to start taking one step at a time.*

The nation itself owns many commercial enterprises, such as the post office. Let the government pass ownership to its current employees and let these employees become self-governing owners of the nation's postal delivery services. This would become a national model for equitable wealth and power distribution. Ultimately, employee ownership of all national and even local services industries would establish a benchmark of economic democracy that could never be overcome by any social or political "ism."

One caution of primary importance — both government and industry have units that employ thousands of workers, and size has the same paralyzing effect on industry as it has in the political sphere. Consequently, equitable employee ownership must always govern democratically from below and never from above. Success will be achieved only by granting the greatest amount of community independence, encouraging local spirit and supporting workplace autonomy. It is thus that employee-owners can be assured a fair and just form of equitable equality.

A completely democratic reorganization of America's power, with social and economic justice as its guiding principle, will affirm the energies already displayed by active environmentalists, equal rights advocates, and racial minorities who have deep seated aspirations towards their perceived segment of liberty. They now must become aware that their goals can be even more quickly achieved if they will acknowledge one principle that they have so far ignored — an equitable return of the nation's power to its Ultimate Sovereign. Only then will all the people achieve their goals.

Be reminded: the financial forces of plutocratic capitalism are tightly focused on methodically shattering our loyalties. Grassroots politics, already weakened, must not be allowed to fail. Often it is less than twenty percent of registered voters who consider local governing issues worth a journey to the polls. Millions have not bothered to even register to vote. In national elections, the selections of our reigning Legal Sovereigns are being decided by far less than one-half of the eligible electorate.

At a more personal level, when a voter ignores the local politics that control important issues like property zoning and the quality of local education, our so-called equal rights becomes an even more empty shell. Land speculators and commercial interests with axes to grind will use undercover payments and secret kickbacks in a multitude of devious ways, to impose economic control over local officials and local affairs.

This unacceptable condition exists only because it is being accepted, endorsed, and perpetuated by our own apathetic indifference. If we cannot learn to deal with political responsibility within our local community, it stands to reason that we cannot hope to ever achieve it nationally.

National Organization

The case for a complete recovery and redistribution of this nation's political power is overwhelming. Yes, we do need a national government to handle foreign policy and deal with national and international affairs, but only at the highest level and only within that responsibility.

But a smaller regionally assigned government, perhaps seven or nine divisions representing individual or combined States in accordance with population or geographical district separations, should be created. This would free the clogged machinery of multi-level centralized bureaucracies, creating new and valuable spheres for democracy in action. Then, we would not be self-driven to political apathy by the belief that we are an utterly powerless speck in a decaying mass.

If, along with employee-ownership of government and community services and all commercial industries, we were to also establish politically responsible regions, we will have originated the most efficient democracy ever devised. Each citizen would have an elected body to deal with his interests, and these varied interests could easily be disentangled.

An example will make this clear: Let us make a case around John Smith, a postal employee living in Weirton, West Virginia. He would by right of his vote have a share in the control of Weirton, in the county of Hancock, in the state of West Virginia, in the region of Appalachia (if it is found desirable to divide America into regions), in the United States, and thereby, all global decisions that America becomes involved in.

In addition, as an employee-owner, he would be entitled to his say about leadership at his own post office station, and in the branch of postal work in which he is involved. He would be self-represented at his local post office, in his regional postal authority, and as part of national operations he would even have a say in international postal involvement. He would share in the activities of on-site workplace democracy by his selection of local leaders, and they in turn, at each progressive upward level as well.

If he became an active political party representative, he could find ways to express his views not only on local issues but also on state, regional and national concerns as well. Then he might also participate in a club or friendly society, in a veterans group, in a religious or perhaps secular society, or he might even become interested in expanding his education by attending readily available free classes.

If power distribution, carried to this almost feverish pitch, does not make John Smith realize that democracy is something more than a neglected title, then democracy should be permanently laid to rest along with Mr. Smith's personal liberty and his individual rights.

Such an outline of possibilities will give rise to obvious criticisms from the in-power capitalists. John Smith, they will argue, is merely an average American. While he is capable of dying in a war, he is incapable of handling himself as a totally free man.

Besides, he is already happy working as a wage-slave for forty hours a week — or perhaps only thirty-two or twenty-four if society ever manages to organize its efforts more efficiently. This citizen comes home tired at the end of his day, or he may even like to stop for a beer with his friends at the neighborhood bar. Or perhaps, our Mr. Smith is married and a father, and he likes to spend quality time with his family. His only interest is in his home, not in the nation. In any event, Smith only wants to enjoy his basically simple pleasures, and he is at this point comparatively satisfied, so why would he even want to change the existing system?

Further, they will say, such a man as Mr. Smith does not want to be bothered with the eternal parade of candidates, committees, and elections that a redistribution of the nation's power would thrust upon him. He simply will not expend the energy necessary to follow up on all the various interests we have described. In fact, he may, as he has in the past, become sick of the whole thing and simply refuse to go near the ballot box. In short, Smith is simply not interested in exchanging his media-conditioned, couch-potato apathy for the demands of public meeting activity. Therefore, they would conclude, these extremely valid reasons favor continuation of unfettered slavery under America's existing capitalistic plutocracy.

Somehow, their argument is not a picture of either a free society or a nation that any American should be proud of. Actually, no one would expect every citizen to take a deep interest or even an active part in all of the manifold concerns of society. Some will prefer one aspect of life, some another. John Smith's interests may actually be centered on his postal work, his growing family, and his interest in sports. While Doris Brown, a co-worker, is vitally concerned with the local zoning laws, administration of the educational system or other uncaring government errors in her city, or even at the state or national level.

The vital point is, the democratic process releases our free will participation in the common good, and each one of us can thereby feel self-governing. Democracy is thus the curse and blessing of individual responsibility.

At this point, it is obvious that no amount of constitutional enticements can force John Smith or any other citizen to go to the polls if he prefers to waste his leisure time. But it is equally obvious that every John Smith and Doris Brown can practice democracy if they want to.

It is Them vs. Us

An equitable redistribution of political power may sound infinitely complex and, simultaneously, infinitely dangerous. It may lead us to complete confusion on the question of constitutional sovereignty and route us too near some other diluted form of an equally uncontrollable bureaucracy. But a national goal of equitable human equality, combined with social and economic justice for all, demands our attention.

When we are willing to accept the risks and attempt recovery of our individual and collective rights within our communities and our workplace, we are at least following one irrefutable principle — that democracy, like all good things, begins at home.

Be reminded, the practitioners of rule by wealth are continuously expanding their control by defiantly taking our sovereignty into their own hands. These Wall Street owners of vast confiscated empires know, and have always feared, that we would one day find our right to dignity in the equitable human equality that would naturally flow from a true democracy.

We are at a true crossroad. It is truly them vs. us, and direct action is necessary. For their lobbyists are wielding powerful financial leverage upon government at every level, and they must be stopped.

American craftsmanship has already been thrown away by the export of millions of new-wealth creating manufacturing jobs, purely to increase corporate profits. Now even our middle-class pride is rapidly disappearing. Their final solution is outsourcing, assuring the decline and fall of the American Empire.

Accordingly, the nation must undergo a course of constructive change. We have no desires against the concept of a national government. Indeed, it is an imperative necessity with national and global affairs moving as rapidly as they are.

But here and now, we must demand our democratic right to an equitable human equality, for this is the only way to safeguard against special interest tyranny. Together, we must search for and find a way to get beyond their pervasive materialistic greed. A principal case for making democracy a reality in our-America.

What an opportunity! A tremendous task, easily accomplished, if we merely stop accepting political rhetoric and set our nation's house in order. As American citizens, we have a duty to help in the rescue of our-America from the destructive forces of plutocratic capitalism that now threaten it.

One whisper joined with another, and then another — can become a shout that is heard by everyone who is discontent with what we have become.

Democracy may not be the perfect solution, but it does hold tremendous future potential. If, that is, We, the People, are to have a future.

CHAPTER 13
NOW IS THE TIME

> *Help achieve democracy or fight against it, but for the nation's sake do not ignore it.*

Here and now, We, the People, have surrendered to work forever more, as wage-slaves. While our mind is being overwhelmed with endless demands on our flag-waving patriotism, Wall Street continues to expand its search for the very last drop of sweat from our brow. While we are mumbling about "liberty and justice for all", they are continuing their government-approved confiscation of all they can steal.

The truth is, too many Americans keep thinking democracy is the mainstay of our nation's existence. We often hear, "Democracy is the only way to go." Yet these same people, so ready to fight and die for the principles of our non-existent democracy, are hypocrites. Though they cry out in muffled praise, they are themselves incapable of describing the benefits that would flow from a real democracy in their own nation.

When the politicians ask, "Are we better off today than we were yesterday?" The answer is not important, for the real question is, "Will today advance us toward any of our expectations?"

If we are to ever have our-America, we must embark upon a serious self-examination concerning what we need to get started. Clearly, we cannot hope to achieve our objective unless we restrict the scope of our investigation.

Democracy in our-America will happen only when a more equitable form of human equality becomes the bonding principle of our common existence — a state of mutual esteem and respect for the rights of all the people.

With so pinnacled an objective, we must restrict our considerations to a full recovery of democracy's three primary needs: 1) the people's free will, 2) the common good, and 3) our individual responsibility. These headings describe the essentials necessary to exercise our Ultimate Sovereignty. While other needs may suggest other ideals, democracy, once achieved, will allow us the freedom to search as far as we please.

The People's Free Will

Democracy, as we have shown, is direct participation by the people in support of their Legal Sovereign. Therefore, the first need we speak of is the people's free will. It is not the same as the nation's free will, though Wall Street would have it be so.

Be reminded, it is through our own apathy and ignorance that we have unknowingly surrendered our free will to their-rule by the confiscated wealth they have taken from us. Through their corporate controlled media, they continually flood our senses with distorted news and calculated rhetoric, maintaining our submissive acceptance and thereby confirming their right to command.

This ever-present abuse of our free will is detrimental to every aspect of our individual existence. And, it is this nearly dormant factor of democracy that makes it an absolute requirement as the first of our primary needs.

At this point we must again confront the subjective vs. objective functions of all politicians. While campaigning for political office all candidates expound upon their ability to serve the people better, only because the other guy is worse. While we are naively casual about the electoral process, they are deadly serious about being in command.

They rightfully contend that once elected, they legally possess the people's free will and it is theirs to use or abuse. And from this point on, watching their lips means nothing, only their actions will bring it on.

Historically the only requirement we ask of America's elected officials is that they will protect and serve our interests. Non-aggression and an adequate existence have been the people's basic goal, and once this minimum is met that is the end of it. From this passive-submissive attitude, the Republicrats have rightly assumed that the people will accept any carefully measured promise, delivered or not. This kind of blind patriotic allegiance and obedience is the "final solution" of all whom would be king.

Denial of access to the truth, at all levels of social, economic and political reality, is the basis of Wall Street's power over our free will. By purchasing control of the Washington Republicrats, special interest lobbyists now dictate our national policies. Collectively, they have gutted this nation's environmental laws, tax laws, securities laws and trade laws in order to directly benefit Wall Street capitalists.

If the core justification for the very existence of government is efficient public service, every closed-door private meeting violates the free will and rights of all the people. For practitioners of democracy any attempt at weakening the citizen's free will violates our individual rights and thereby creates an immediate demand for corrective action. An open and honest administration must fully and fairly represent the citizen's free will or face the consequences.

Take particular notice: when either of this nation's main political parties gain administrative control of any branch of their-government, it maintains its hold by creating an image of superior expertise, special insider knowledge that only those in their magic circle can perform. Not limited to Republican or Democrat, conservative or liberal, hawk or dove, left or right, their words are always accompanied by a Republicratic contempt for our individual rights, and complete disregard for any social or economic justice for all the people. It is through this kind of distorted ideology that this plutocracy has kept democracy out of our hands.

Periodically, a true believer will declare a personal brand of supreme wisdom, to justify some unconstitutional action that is in the best self-interest of their nation. Both Julius Caesar and Adolph Hitler established dictatorial regimes to "restore order," and thereby created an armed security force that killed off millions. Here and now, Bush's Patriot Act, when intertwined with his subsequent preemptive invasions and occupations, may be a precursor to something far worse. While the initial effort may produce some professed result, what may follow is a fanaticism that can lead to self-destruction and eventual ruin.

In his time, the New Deal years of Franklin Delano Roosevelt came very close to a figurative dictatorship in America. The American people, exhausted by the Great Depression, gladly ceded their powers of self-direction to a man that never shrank from his responsibility. Political power was heaped upon FDR to a near breaking point.

There was a voluntary surrendering of our free will for self-government, a temporary tolerance of dictatorial methods, so beneficial to the masses that he in fact, became president for life. Interestingly, this New Deal and World War II period in American history became an entrenchment of government bureaucracy from which we have still not recovered.

The truth is, happiness for the people truly depends upon the way our free will is exercised and the degree of our public participation in government. Communities, in concert with its citizens, are always better off when they self-govern. Passing their local problems ever upward to city, state and national government merely produces added levels of bureaucracy. Only local involvement and action from within the area in question assures the will of the people will be done. Hence, democracy will prevail.

Note that democratic principles always return to the merit of individual values, to govern ourselves as best we can, or passively sit back and have it done for us. The option is always conditioned by the degree of logic that supports the objective.

Building a bridge over a raging river requires skilled engineers and there can be no excuse for not hiring expert builders. The decision to build the bridge however must come from those who will use the bridge — not from the Republicrats who will never use it but will make you pay double for your having made the request.

It is the end, not the means, that must determine the kind of life that a community should strive for. Only the collective free will of the people should determine this nation's governing policies, and the final choice is a cerebral, almost spiritual, matter —our-humanity and our-democracy as one entity.

Thus, a government of, by, and for the people, must be a collective commitment of our free will. It should serve our common needs through a fairly elected representative body. If apathy is an individual's choice, we are at liberty to be apathetic.

On the other hand, if we choose to be a responsible, free thinking person, we may work and sweat to achieve greater goals, and should we succeed our pleasure will far outstrip our past wage-slavery and mere feeding at the public welfare trough.

Whose free will should we fight for? Theirs, or ours? I am but one. It is only when you join your free will with mine that we can turn this Republic of States into a Democracy of Human Beings.

The Common Good

Every successful division by any economic, social, moral, religious, or racial measurement becomes, in a true sense, a death knell for democracy. It will only be through an equitable allocation of the common good that democracy can deliver "liberty and justice for all".

Think about it. When we collectively accept the concept of a truly equitable human equality, we are simultaneously dispensing sovereignty and allocating earned power among the people. And thereby, we accept our right to individually share in the common good.

At present, not even an outer shell of the common good can be seen within this nation's plutocratic society. The secretive social class war, now going on throughout America, is as fatal to our primary ideals as the hatred generated by racial prejudice or religious domination. When confiscated wealth is used as a weapon to promote and expand inequality, it makes our pretended democracy a farce of the first magnitude.

Any government that legalizes subservient wage-slavery and forces 35-million of its citizens to live in poverty, has no right to even speak of democracy let alone lay claim to being its champion. It is thus that our pretense of democracy is worth nothing when Washington Republicrats can so easily limit or restrict in any way the common good, for this has in turn destroyed liberty and justice by its creation of societal inequality.

Many well-intentioned people have argued that it is possible for the rich and the poor to be friends. Perhaps, but not if this friendship is based on wage-slave servitude. The master cannot accept the slave as his friend and equal, lest by happenstance their places be exchanged.

Be reminded, every form of slavery dishonors labor. It numbs our physical abilities and mental capacities, and it stifles our creative talents. What else must I say to awaken your individuality? Is it possible you do not care that you are indeed, still a slave? Unfettered and paid wages yes, but only because it proved unprofitable to forever house and feed you and maintain your chains.

How can we even speak of a quality of life in America, unless each citizen has free access to an equality of lifestyle? If human need includes any sense of the common good, then individuals can only be free if they fully reject every priority on materialistic domination.

A sense of the common good for all is a challenge that must be met. For without it, we can never establish and then cherish this vision called democracy.

Be reminded, the economic power of wealth now holds complete control over our humanity. We can only change this vile tradition by exercising our free will and instilling an entirely new kind of morality into our consciousness, one that will naturally favor the common good, a major objective. And, "When the students have assembled, the teachers will appear."

More than ever, our hope for an enduring democracy in America can only come from an enlightened next generation. This will require us to reach beyond the way it is, with our excessive supply of mini-kingdom morality, where our individual right to democracy cannot be found.

The solution will require a common sense move towards cooperation instead of competition, and we know the difference. Here and now it is time for an all out fight to establish democracy in our-America. It will not be a fair fight. Wall Street has its confiscated accumulation of old-wealth, and all we have is the Ultimate Sovereign power of We, the People.

We can begin our activities in the workplace, talking with each other about the benefits of a real democracy, and voluntarily taking on tasks that will serve our common interests. This will be one small step of one giant leap toward improving everyone's lifestyle.

Only by working together can we better our own lives, and make our-America better as well. There will be some that will try to take advantage of the very basis of our cooperation, but on the whole we will all be better off. The synergy of individuals in cooperation with each other will become an unstoppable force.

A free will association of people, who unite in the common good of all, will create a natural morality that will transcend the widely varying beliefs of all individuals who make up the group. And within every group a natural leadership will emerge, one of its own choosing, one that does not pander to special interests, one that ensures that democracy, once achieved, will last forever.

Only an honest openness within a cooperative community will naturally welcome those who have been kept isolated. The existence of common purpose will bring out loyalties and activities that the vacuum of isolation has destroyed. Cooperative purpose in our leisure and in our work, based on loyalty to the nation and a constant challenge to our abilities, will be a valued stimulant.

Any community or nation which fosters cooperation, in concert with its free will towards common goals, would thus be far happier than one bound by the monotonous and barren creed of rule by the power of wealth. Democracy is the natural outcome of majority action, and its practice of the common good will affirm a democracy that will last forever.

Whose common good should we fight for? Theirs, or ours? I am but one, it is only when you join your need for the common good with mine that we can turn this Republic of States into a Democracy of Human Beings.

Our Individual Responsibility

Wall Street's economic manipulations (backed by political control of the masses) are vital to the continuation of their One World economy. While they may occasionally provide the people with some marginal benefit, an involuntary spill from their overflowing horn of plenty, you can be assured it will be paid for with more deregulation and another tax cut from their Republicratic friends

On the other hand, people within a democracy place a greater value on our-humanity than on their-profit. The former thinks only in terms of the power of confiscated wealth, the latter only in terms of individual rights. Common sense dictates that we should think in the political terms of both. Economic and social concerns are complimentary, not conflicting.

Our free will and the common good are of little value unless we take the time to fully understand the meaning and function of our individual responsibility. Our right to vote, for instance, without the ability to comprehend the issues at hand, is no guarantee of freedom or liberty. Doing far worse damage are the non-registered and non-voters, convinced by the corporate controlled media that they couldn't make a difference.

Take notice — special interests no longer even try to block voter registration, because they know the right to vote means nothing when the voter can be so easily influenced by a corporate controlled manipulating media blitz. Only a properly informed voter makes any real difference at the ballot box.

When the majority of the people can be kept ignorant or made receptive to any given message, the people's power can never be realized. And therefore, the nation's power remains in the hands of those who can financially manipulate the public's opinion at will.

The one force that can guarantee true democracy for every American citizen is education. By this we do not mean education only for those who can afford it. There must be free education for all that are motivated.

When any of our children are not adequately prepared or competently instructed, the inevitable outcome is failure through their ignorance of available opportunities. Through a full and free education, we intend development of everyone's critical powers, equipping each with enough knowledge to naturally create a healthy skepticism about any and every excess.

For as long as we are willing to bend to the empty-headed symbols of plutocracy, Wall Street's word wizards will keep their hold on America's throne. Only when every individual within the majority begins to responsibly question government deception will hope dawn for all of us. Only when Education + Opportunity + Ownership = Human Dignity for all, will We, the People, finally win.

What must be done to stop us from waiting for someone else to act? Continued false promises and faked goodwill can not and will not save us. Until the majority of the nation's people have access to the truth, combined with the skill and ability to understand it, there will be no liberty in which the mind of man can have a free choice.

The truth is, in our-America, the nation's teachers alone could, and they must, insist on a full development of our most valuable resource, the American mind. There is, however, nothing more frustrating than our present system of education by memorization, a tossing of textbooks at the student with an admonishment to "learn" in time for a test.

This archaic habit perpetuates the Plutocrats' preference for deceptive words. Every subject distorted, to exchange the objectives of human concern for the benefits of materialistic possession. To memorize a plethora of ill-digested and frequently distorted information will certainly fill the student's time. But will it fill his mind?

It has been argued that without programmed memorization some students wouldn't learn anything. I would argue that if each learns only his own ignorance, and is taught to know what he does not know, he is on the road to knowledge. Only when we first learn to free our individual self from the false idols of unfair and unbalanced phraseology can we then set out to discover the truth.

By simply working together, we can automatically start a responsible movement towards an education that will make all words meaningful and all issues clear. Clouded thinking will be forever gone when every student and teacher cooperatively demands that education become an endless search for truth and reality.

Education + Opportunity + Ownership = Human Dignity, is the formula for success. It is a guarantee that these boys and girls, who will become America's men and women, can and will build a free society where the right to choose is fortified by a well-informed capacity to choose.

This liberty of thought will enhance free and powerful thinking. Be reminded, any irresponsible society that cripples itself and then remains incapacitated, must never forget that its suffering is self-inflicted.

Only a real democracy can assure that its citizens will be enabled to think for themselves. To have an uneducated democracy is indeed a contradiction in terms. For the power to rule will remain only with those who, having knowledge, can manufacture public opinion at will.

Democracy demands attention and all must perform unremitting and continuous maintenance. "The price of liberty is eternal vigilance," and eternal vigilance is a major burden to place upon our individual responsibility.

Whose individual responsibility should we account for? Theirs, or ours? I am but one. It is only when you join your individual responsibility with mine that this Republic of States will become a Democracy of Human Beings.

CHAPTER 14

AMERICA

> *Shaped by our-humanity, deformed by their-greed*

In an endless battle for more power, and the right to use it, we collectively form into productive occupations that will house and feed ourselves in our brief journey between life and death. Choosing between what is necessary and what is available, we continually arrive at new points of decision and acceptance — to stay the way we are, or go on to become the best that we can be.

Unfortunately, within each and every one of us, our instinct to survive demands a bit more "want" than we really need. This leads to greed, which unbalances someone else's quality of life. Should all of us give in to greed, the battle will be endless and few would survive

The who, what, when, why and how of this nation and its people, must become a continuous work in progress. We must forever change as wants and needs rise and fall in constant evolution toward an inevitable end of perfection or extermination.

Thus America, like every other nation, is nothing but a collection of natural and human resources, living through a cycle of life. None asking to be born, but once here, fighting to survive and willing to compete. Constantly generating new energy, every thought, word or deed impacted by the power of friend or foe. We are a synergy of the social, economic and political motivations of the people, combining and separating in a process of creation, possession and ownership that defines power but does not control it. Which leaves us to ask, and answer:

Who is in charge? We are! Why are we here? To perfect our own existence. What do we want? To be the best that we can be. How can we get there? By working together. When will we start? Now would be a good time. Who is stopping us? We are!

By the first three words of this nation's Constitution, We, the People, are empowered to individually and collectively choose political freedom or containment. Thus we become what we allow. Our governing system expanding or contracting our existence, swinging like a pendulum, too far one way, before going too far the other.

While we are simply searching for our own perfection, they are pushing and pulling us into an elastic-walled prison. We now find ourselves more contained than free, trapped by a political/economic distortion, a plutocratic efficiency, valuing their ever higher profits by forever lowering our humanity. Yet, by simply reversing this priority, placing our-humanity before their-profit, we can finally break free.

In what is now their-America, one-percent are very rich, twelve-percent are very poor, and the rest of us are passive-submissive subservient wage-slave drones. Yet, as this nation's Ultimate Sovereigns, We, the people, can instantly fix this distortion and balance this ratio. By our right to vote we can create a democracy. An equitable human equality, best demonstrated by simply admitting what we have isn't equitable.

Human dignity, our end goal — determined by acquired knowledge, advantaged by opportunity, and measured by ownership—is created by this natural association, one with another, asking and answering our common need for continuing education, protection from harm and readily available public services.

If this nation's managers stayed tightly focused on just these primary elements, there would be no problems. But greed will always rise, when we lower our own dignity through apathy. The rich will get richer, the poor will get poorer, and we everyday Americans will either watch the decline and fall of this Republic of States, or witness the rise of a Democracy of Human Beings.

CHAPTER 15

THE END

> *Or, is it the Beginning?*

The following are some of my more specific thoughts and ideas for a troubled America. They are offered with mixed feelings of concern, apprehension, and hope: concern about the very survival of our-America. Apprehension because our need for a real democracy is so desperate as to be nearly ominous. And hope that together, We, the People, will turn this Republic of States into a Democracy of human Beings.

There are three problems that most Americans can at least partially agree with: Wall Street greed is threatening our very existence, unemployment and poverty are major problems, and the best government that money can buy has made too many promises to too many special interests. Here, We, the People, need to ask, and answer: Is now the time to set ourselves free from their elastic-walled prison of partisan politics and financial manipulations?

Jobs

For too many, the long-heralded "American Dream" has become an ever-threatening nightmare of closed factories, lost jobs, eliminated pensions, and no medical coverage. We, the People, have been lulled into import-mania, media-conditioned to buy more and more imported products on easy credit, so Wall Street's robber-barons can live on Easy Street.

In 1947, 37 percent of America's workforce were directly involved in the creation of new wealth, manufacturing, everything from shoelaces to ocean liners. Today, this number is less than 9 percent. Where once we were the biggest and best, today we are little more than an also-ran.

America's net worth is now being transferred abroad at an alarming rate. For the last thirty-four continuous year's, Wall Street profiteers have been cutting their costs by exporting our jobs and adding to our misery. This has created an ever-increasing and accumulating international trade deficit, now more than five trillion dollars.

Will you take a moment and simply connect the dots? When Wall Street imports more than they export, we are consuming more than we are producing. It doesn't take much thought to realize this is a self-depleting reality. At some point our cupboard will be bare. Is this a continuing saga in the decline and fall of the American Empire.

Do you think I'm crying wolf? Well, just answer this question: What's in your closet? Look at the labels and tell me how many of them say Made in USA? Next, check your appliances, electronics, and your garage. What percentage of your stuff was made by a hands-on American?

Now tell me. Are you willing to help fix the problem? You don't have to join anything, contribute any money, or give up any of your pleasures or treasures. All you have to do is NOT buy any imported products on the first day of every month of every year until the end of time. I'm asking you to be a red white and blue patriot once a month. "Think outside the box" for just a minute. What will happen if 285 million Americans unite in this one single purpose? On this one day of every month, of every year, until the end of time, Washington and Wall Street will be put on notice, to start caring now, about the future of our-America

Taxation

The subject of taxation in America is a 15,000 page quagmire of complexity, where more or less of one kind of tax or another is of no importance, when the best government that money can buy is writing the rules. Do you really believe they're thinking about us when they are writing laws that might adversely affect their own privileged status or the status of Wall Street interests that will gladly pay for an incumbent's next political campaign?

Did you know that corporate and other hidden income taxes currently make up 20% to 30% of all retail prices? It's true. These hidden taxes are passed on to the consumer in the form of higher prices, from 20% to 30% higher than they would otherwise be for everything you buy.

Therefore, by replacing our current income-based tax system, with a fair consumer-based tax system, consumer prices will automatically drop 20% to 30%. Then, instead of sending (an average of 28% in income taxes, plus 15.3% in payroll taxes) a total of 43% of your paycheck to the Republicrats in Washington, you will take home 100% of your paycheck, and pay only a 24% consumption tax each time you purchase a new good or service for your own personal consumption. If you choose to buy used goods you do not pay any tax at all.

At this 24% rate, this fair tax will pay for all current government operations, including Social Security, Medicare, and a single payer national health plan. Government revenues will be even more stable than they are now because this nation's economy is more accurately measured by its consumption than by its inequitable distribution of income.

Perhaps most importantly, to ensure that no American will pay tax on necessities, a fair tax plan would provide a prepaid, monthly rebate for every registered household to cover the 24% consumption tax spent on necessities up to the federal poverty level. This is how a fair tax would completely un-tax the poor, and lower the tax burden on everyone else as well. Can you see how much freer life will be with a fair tax instead of an unfair income tax?

If you like this concept, tell the Washington Republicrats to pass HR25/S1493, the Fair Tax Act of 2003. Want more information? Go to... **fairtax.org**

EDUCATION

In today's America, we expect 100% perfection in every product or service that we buy. But from our schools we're getting less than half of what we're paying for. One-fourth of students drop out, and another one-fourth graduate barely able to read their own diplomas.

My fellow Americans, despite hundreds of glib promises and media grabbing headlines, politicians, government officials, business and educational leaders have all failed in their efforts to improve our schools. They fail because they keep trying to fix a system that simply isn't working, and it hasn't worked for a very long time. It fails because it judges success by a collective average rather than an individual's success or failure. And the average they use is based on the worst of the best, and the best of the worst, a completely unacceptable standard.

While two-thirds of adult Americans do have at least a high school diploma and more than one-fifth has completed college, the nation's average intelligence is actually declining. These statistics confirm the poor job that is being done. The Department of Education is neither improving the quantity or the quality of knowledge coming out of our schools and universities. To change this reality, students will need more hours in the classrooms and in the gym, and far less hours watching TV and gobbling up fast food

In my mind, there is no question that every American has the ability to learn. But the question that does haunt me is: Can every person perform equally on varying subjects, at the same time, on the same required level?   Well, in case you haven't guessed, the answer is NO.

Just as everyone cannot be a great artist, everyone cannot be a rocket scientist. Our entire educational system needs to be focused on advancing each student by his or her sequential mastery of each subject, rather than on some chronological grade level.

To accomplish this goal we will need teachers who can create the kinds of tasks for students that will encourage them to expand their thinking, and not just prompt them to provide cut-and-dried answers, to cut-and-dried questions. We need an educational system that leads rather than manages, one that stresses discipline, motivation, and achievement.

More than just getting a passing grade or receiving a diploma, students must be challenged to maximize their individual capabilities. And then, using this broader base of raw knowledge, they can and will pose insightful questions, invent new products, create new art, explore untested ideas, and organize all of the resources necessary to complete these tasks.

To end this terrible waste of human potential we must put an end to the K-12 grade level system. Reading, writing, mathematics and all the social and natural sciences are subjects that are learned at varying speeds, set by each individual's interests and abilities.

There is far more value in fully developing our children's individual ability to be problem solvers, rather than dropout problem makers. Starting from the bedrock of life itself, we need to add layer upon layer of ever-advancing educational success. Only as a fully informed individual can every American enter the portal of opportunity, into a world of satisfying work and earned leisure, a just reward for a job well done

The Ways and Means

Building our-America will require a political regrouping of our combined natural and human resources. Cutting the cord between present owners and what would be the new employee-owners must be through a legitimate process, a fair exchange of new wealth for old equity. Through a political resolution of natural and human resource ownership, We, the People, can get on with the job of building our-America.

Financed by a new Federal Reserve banking system, an equally new Capital Homestead Act can identify and then allocate the ways and means of economic democracy. Programs will include, employee stock ownership of all new wealth creating manufacturers; community consumer stock ownership of all utility, support and service facilities; national employee stock ownership of organizations that are vital to the population at large.

The size and shape of these employee-owned operations are to be determined by a natural economy of scale — the highest and best use of natural and human resources. We will never take more than we need, and never need more than we make.

This will require a collective agreement of humanity before profit. A three way accommodation between Wall Street, Washington and We, the People, creating and meeting a demand that plutocracy ends and democracy begins. A tough job, an absolute transition, that must start here and now!

Want more information on the varying kinds of employee ownership and a Capital Homestead Act? Go to **cesj.org** The Center for Social and Economic Justice have been fighting this battle for equitable equality for many years, and they have the know-how to make it work.

IN SUMMARY...

Democracy in America. It is a complete illusion, a pretentious spectacle, preached like a "sermon from the mount," yet few people have taken the time to understand its message, or bother themselves about the loss of their natural rights as a human being.

The truth is, only reality and change are life's toughest obstacles. Should We, the People, decide to go for democracy, you will not be asked to abandon your home, leave your job or family, but instead you are invited to become a force for change from within. There is no call for war or revolution, for who will fight if we all agree?

We have a choice — servitude or freedom, uncontrolled secrecy or open knowledge, selected poverty or mutual prosperity. Democracy has only one requirement. We must all pull together on an up hill journey, with only a promise of a fantastic view from the top... **our-America.**

EPILOGUE

A conclusion of cause and effect, worthy of change.

The 3rd Millennium

Each successive millennium tends toward radical shifts in the prevailing paradigm. Pre-Christian eras are notable for searching, finding, and choosing the pathways that humanity has followed. The first millennium (0-1000 AD) contributed a hodgepodge of social mythology and political theories that evolved into organized religions and disorganized nations, whose wars and acts of terrorism continue to this day.

The second millennium included the dark ages, the age of enlightenment, and the industrial age. Each age, persuading a life of progressively increasing self-interest, continually reinforcing the fear that friend and foe alike will take an unfair advantage.

Currently, with automation and ever-advancing technology replacing hands-on craftsmanship, a middle-class dependency on wage-slavery and incorporate servitude now prevails. Is it any wonder that so many underpaid and badly housed Americans are driven to family failure and total despair by the socially brutal economic forces which dominate today's America?

There is much to be changed if indeed the words We, the People, are to have any meaning in this third millennium. The nation is larger, the population is greater, and the quality of wants and the quantity of needs have expanded far beyond the wildest dreams of this nation's founders. Should we rely upon a more than two-century old constitution as anything more than a good beginning?

A Call to Arms

My instincts tell me, now is the time to explore a new and more viable alternative for this nation's political and economic policies. The people's unspoken questions need answers; the unanswerable questions need options.

The truth is, our America's natural and human resources are being consumed by a Wall Street tyranny of rule-by-wealth. Taking an unfair advantage of our willingness to go along, in order to get along, the people have been sucked into a quicksand of unjust laws and inequitable taxation. An unending reality of financial greed and political corruption — fueled by our own apathy — has destroyed our common sense of right and wrong, what being an American is all about.

There is a real need for us to agree that it's okay to do the right thing. And, while its okay to say, you don't know what to do. It's not okay to say you don't care. Giving in to yesterday, must never be confused with giving up on tomorrow.

The primary question is, has the best government that money can buy abandoned We, the People? And, the answer is yes! But fixing this problem is not a matter of political revolution, social retribution, or economic redistribution.

We need more than a change

The Supreme Court selection of George W Bush as their president has constitutionally confirmed the absence of democracy in our America, proving the people cannot win. Which forces me to ask why we are putting up with this plutocracy, this absolute rule by the power of wealth? And the answer is, unless and until we demand an end to both Wall Street greed and Main Street poverty, a sustainable society is improbable and democracy is impossible.

Far more capable now than we were in 1776, We, the People, must demand a government guarantee that every American will be well-housed, adequately clothed, competitively educated, and productively employed.

Here I submit a new social-contract theory, a governing political/economic philosophy called Democratism, a democratic rule by the majority as a far more acceptable companion for economic capitalism than this nation's current system, a plutocratic minority that rules by the power of confiscated wealth.

By definition, capitalism is a measurable economic system, politically empowered to commodify everything from bottled water to human body parts. Who will profit is determined by the nation's choice of governing political policies. Only when the economics of capitalism run parallel with the greater good of a political democracy will the words We, the People, have real meaning.

The prime directive of Democratism (democratic-capitalism) is to expose the wrongs of self-serving wealth and power, replacing them with the rights of human dignity. When we, the powerless, are no longer exploited and divided by the powerful, we can then measure our progress in terms of the common good, not by the betterment of some to the detriment of others. Only people can create new wealth, and wealth must never again become our master.

The journey from our presently competitive society, to a fully cooperative one, is purely a matter of acknowledging the priority of humanity before profit. Any politician who is not willing to accept this human priority is obviously out of step with the people's interests.

Make Your Choice

Democratism, a more humane political economy, will require a new faith in humanity and democracy as one entity. In today's government, too many positions of public trust have become little more than openings for special interest privilege and a dictatorial morality. The only way We, the People, can ever win is to both start and complete — the construction of our America — a task that could take centuries, or one election.

Let the in-office republicrats who want to continue the politics of rule by wealth join or stay in the Republican Party. We, the People, can simply take over the Democratic Party, and then choose and elect new representatives, who will install democratism as this nation's governing (political/economic) philosophy. Backed by the power of the majority, we will then construct our America, and thereby enforce our Constitutional right to "life, liberty, and the pursuit of happiness."

Interestingly, exposing the plutocratic government we have has also exposed a new prime theory of value: The dignity-of-ownership is the genesis of all value.

Confirming our rights as human beings, this theory challenges all of history, the lost ethics, bent morality, political corruption, and economic greed of all that has ever been. Like our natal instinct to root, suck, and grasp, our dignity-of-ownership must become a natural birthright, neither burdened nor advantaged by any unnatural laws of confiscation or inheritance.

Stop overlooking the obvious

Unless and until this nation's governing process is required to serve all the people, we will be forever subservient to enforced social and economic inequities from Washington Republicrats. On this point Democratism may even be called a new Emancipation Proclamation. By recognizing our birthright to knowledge, opportunity and ownership, and thereby our human dignity, every American will finally be released from subservient wage-slavery. Words that until now only spoke of "life, liberty, and the pursuit of happiness," will be affirmed by an enforcement of a more equitable form of human equality.

The truth is, if we simply get rid of the republicrats who've been ripping us off, we're bound to come out ahead. We can kick-start Democratism by demanding an immediate solution for America's four basic problems: 1) A national health plan; 2) free education, as much as we are individually capable of absorbing; 3) an opportunity to be productive on our own behalf, and; 4) secure borders. These are the minimal obligations of any responsible government. Regardless of constant yammering from the republicratic right and left, an unhealthy, under-educated, unemployable, over-populated nation is a threat that must not be ignored.

Means and Ends

No individual, political body, or nation-state has ever faced so complex a human rights issue, a fair and just blending of the means of equity and the ends of equality, and there is nothing to compare this dilemma to. Somehow, We, the People, must find a way to harmonize our nation's values within a sense of the public good, an altruism that nourishes a sustainable society; not a selfishness that feeds on the poverty it perpetuates.

The unlimited opportunities of wide-open frontiers and people striving to be free were the building blocks of early America. But this unheralded opportunity for We, the People, — to have the American Dream — was turned into a nightmare of vast social-class inequities, a tyranny of rule-by-wealth that is now our nemesis. An endless demand for increased Wall Street's profits, regardless of the costs to our humanity.

The-truth is, America's industrial revolution is over and We, the People, lost. The machines of rule by wealth have overrun the individual rights of human beings. The worlds richest one-percent already own or control more than eighty-percent of our America. No longer a means, their-government has become an end unto itself, a ticking bomb of social-class divisiveness, completely out of the people's control.

Our human dignity, like the air we breathe, is unknowable beyond its necessity for life. This genesis of all moral, ethical, and material value is about the life we have, the one that We, the People, can improve. Democratism can, and it must, become our answer to their-government.

We Need Leaders

Leadership, as opposed to management, is often cited as a key factor in successful endeavors. But where do leaders come from? Are they a product of higher education? Is genetic engineering the answer? Should we reach for the brightest and best, and clone their DNA into one supra-standard format? I think not, and I hope not, for it is simply being the right person at the right time that makes leadership apparent and valuable to the rest of us.

The-truth is, it takes good people following better leadership to build the best society. Consider the extremes of recent American Presidents: Jimmy Carter, a domestic uncertainty, has achieved international acclaim. The costs of compounding interest from Ronald Reagan's last acting performance will be an eternal reminder of supply-side idiocy. His cohorts, George

Bush and son will hopefully go down in history as the last warrior presidents, military-industrialists to the bitter end.

Bill Clinton is still the subject of speculation. Will he ever deliver on his potential, an intellectual promise of a higher quality of leadership? All we know for certain is, he tried to lead and we tried to follow, but his message of hope was lost in a moment of personal weakness.

War or Peace

We, the People, must face our toughest enemy, the truth. The Cold War, a test of rule by wealth vs. rule by stealth, was a Wall Street driven fraud. Korea was, and still is an albatross. Vietnam, providing huge profits for the rich and a place to die for the poor, was one of the Republicrats more obvious mistakes. The final costs of the Bush wars on Iraq (a sucker punch by the world's oil barons) are still being tallied.

These Wall Street decisions were all paved with political rhetoric and dead Americans, as were the roads to Somalia, Bosnia, and Afghanistan. These political-industrial games of war contribute to the false belief that America undertakes military action, only to safeguard democracy. But the truth is, America's foreign policy is being written by the demands of a One-World Economy --an international economic dictatorship-- described as good for us?

Should We, the People, be Wall Street's military police force, armed to the teeth, and ever ready to go to war on their behalf? Should American blood be the lubricant that forces the entire world into human subservience to rule by wealth? Must we die, merely to give some headline-seeking republicrat another war drum to beat and another flag to wave?

To politically allow private profiteering on the manufacture and sale of the tools of war is an insult to every American who has ever fought to keep America free. That the people's tax-dollars are ever used to enhance Wall Street profits is an outright fraud.

It is Their-Government

The-truth is, Wall Street's profiteers view their political contributions as simply another written off cost of doing business. Unconcerned that their bribery has decreased the public's rights and increased the national debt, these self-serving capitalists see themselves as an elite class, an unseen power, entitled by their government to decide where and how the wage-slaves will live, and how much we must pay in taxes.

Must we endlessly endure diminishing expectations? Should we, the creators of new wealth, have to pay the cost of benefits for a do-nothing financial elite that recognizes neither human rights nor national allegiance? Should corporate capitalists be allowed to conceal hidden agendas in cloaks of anonymity? Should the wealth of our America be used like a bludgeon, against We, the People? Rooted in early colonialism and 19th century imperialism, 20th century Republicrats have delivered Wall Street's primary objective — an international economic dictatorship.

What an ironic situation, America, the world's bastion of democracy, is itself not a democracy. It is a Republic, ruled by a plutocratic elite. Unless and until We, the People, correct this process, by demanding an equitable equality for every American, today's irony will indeed be tomorrow's tragedy.

The Truth Hurts

Primed by the Wall Street ordered rust-belt debacle of the 1960s, their-government is now abandoning the very last vestiges of pride in American craftsmanship. This early period of planned industrial decay, was closely followed by the insatiable 1980s, the budget busting militarization and deregulation policies of Reagan-Bush. A Wall Street bonanza of uncontrolled junk bond mergers, fattened by pork loaded increases in government spending on weapons we didn't need, bought with money their-government didn't have. This chronic dedication to economic growth and greed is continuing to squander our taxes through a series of pre-emptive wars and long-standing occupations, fueling a continuously expanding and continually growing seven trillion-dollar national debt.

Clinton's misadventures, into NAFTA and GATT, further inspired Wall Street to turn this nation's middle-class administrators, technicians, and planners into another unwanted human surplus. Then, under George W, the Wall Street moguls exported 2-million more manufacturing jobs in their haste to achieve financial dominance over all they can steal. This unbridled rule by wealth has resulted in less real income, less medical care, less education and now a panic of passionate conservative solutions — a whole new round of waste, chaos, and cronyism.

We, the People, must put an end to the republicrats and their faceless special interest corporations. Our dignity-of-ownership must not be bought and sold by financial wizards in *The Wall Street Journal* and, it must not be secretively taken from us by political deceit.

The wealth of this nation is in its natural resources and American ingenuity, the values and craftsmanship of our human resourcefulness. When we produce more than we consume, it is our wealth that must increase. But, if the republicrats continue to legislatively approve the outsourcing of jobs to cheap labor countries, and we continue consuming more goods than we produce, Wall Street's ever-increasing trade deficit will force the nation into the poorhouse.

Grab and Greed

Claiming secretive political/economic alliances are illegally restricting our individual rights and freedoms may sound like a conspiracy. It is!

The problem we common folk have with conspiracy theories is confronting the-truth. Our inner fear of endlessly incredible rhetoric, so obviously false, yet, so extensively organized that in frustration we question our own ability to compete against such an overwhelming force — their-government — the very institution that we thought was established to protect our interests.

If we are to learn anything in this 21st Century, it must be that the grab and greed of rule by wealth is unacceptable in our America. Consider this paradox: Republicrats write the laws that hand to special interests, the power and the wealth that buys the Republicrats.

The bizarre character of this endless conflict, between our recognition of rule-by-wealth and its inhumanity, has produced a deadly disease of instant gratification. A national epidemic of mass marketing, frenzied-finance and artistic-accounting, (Wall Street's transliteration of lie, steal, and cheat,) the credential requirements for a (slave) Masters Degree in Business Administration.

Wake-up America, our tomorrows must never again be limited by inequitable yesterdays. While we've been going to work and paying taxes, they've been robbing the national treasury and destroying our family values. Only by crafting a more democratic form of capitalism can We, the People, even hope to abandon the big lie, a work ethic based on be good, feel guilty, and die poor.

Time to Push Back

This Wall Street mentality of wage-slavery, and increasing foreign ownership, has pushed our America to the brink of economic collapse. Now it is our time to push back. Underemployment is bad, unemployment is worse, but being unemployable is simply unacceptable.

Epilogue

Trapped by multiple layers of taxation and thousands of special exemptions for the rich, the average American is working until mid-April just to pay taxes. To counter this unearned possession of America's wealth and power I have offered — Democratism — a politically enforceable right to a more equitable form of human equality, the ways and means that will put an end to rule by wealth.

This first step toward a sustainable society will require a national administration that delivers our right to knowledge, opportunity, and ownership. We need to restore our common sense, to replace their-government's non-sense.

A second step of recovery may mean cutting the official workweek to 32, or even 24 hours, making a wealth-creating job available for everyone. To some it might seem that 40 hours of labor would be necessary, lest boredom prevail. But, with fewer hours needed for mind-numbing subservience to rule-by-wealth, forced labor simply isn't required to make a sustainable society work.

Only through a community-centered consumer and employee ownership of every business can We, the People, become individually productive on our own behalf. Responsible and accountable, motivated and competent, we will work less hours as employees, yet earn more money as owners. Ultimately, Democratism will naturally eliminate the cause of poverty and the costs of welfare.

A Second Enlightenment

During the first Enlightenment, the truth of science led the common people out of the dark ages of ignorance and mysticism and into an age of human subservience. An ideology of rule by the power of confiscated wealth, that might never have succeeded were it not for religious admonitions to be good, work hard, and be rewarded in an other-world.

This period of Protestant Reformation greatly influenced the nation's founding fathers, and they capitalized the dark-side of their Declaration of Independence by constitutionally prescribing a Republic of States, instead of a Democracy of Human Beings. It is one thing to fondly remember patriotic lessons from the past, it is quite another to be permanently subservient to their purpose-filled distortions.

No state or corporate institution should have the right to limit, deny or suppress human dignity, the gathering of knowledge, opportunity and ownership, the ways and means of life and living. Together, we must expose this nation's pretense of democracy, and it is well within our constitutional right, to demand a second enlightenment, a turning point toward humanity before profit, the greatest challenge any civilization has ever had to confront..

A New Adventure in Democracy

United by common purpose We, the People, must undertake a new adventure in democracy. Politics in our America can no longer be a spectator sport. Voting, more than a right or privilege, must become an obligation of civic responsibility, a price that everyone must eagerly pay for the liberty, justice, and prosperity that we are entitled to. It's our wealth they're wasting, and it's our vote that can stop them. When We, the People, speak democratically, the sound of the majority must never again be ignored.

Taking us far beyond the basic needs of survival, a sustainable society must become a central theme in our sense of well being about our children and our hope for the future. But first we must confront the-truth: Our prosperity is being dashed against the rocks of our own ignorance, for we have allowed a rule by wealth that has created an out-of-control national debt.

We, the People, must refuse to pay these mortgages, placed on our nation's future. And, we must free our children of this debt, lest they revolt against us if we are unable or unwilling to fix the errors we are forcing upon them.

We owe our soul to their company's stores

The-truth is, the machines of the industrial age started it all by replacing human skills with wage-slavery and indentured servitude, an exploitation of child labor and sweat shops filled with overworked and underpaid workers. Invisible-hands, (read; a do-nothing elite,) began their accumulations of capital, (read; human dignity,) assuring the possessions of those that have, against the rights of those who have-not. These now privately held hordes of capital reserves, (read; property and money,) are in fact the unpaid residual values of our forefathers' labor.

In their One-World Economy, nation-state loyalty is of no importance in their never-ending pursuit of profit before humanity. This covert transfer of the public's wealth to private control, greatly enhanced by Reagan-Bush deregulation, is now being further threatened by George W's neurosis-- massive tax cuts for the rich.

A debt responsibility of more than $25,000 for each and every American is our share of their, rapidly increasing, seven trillion-dollar national debt. This obviously failed result of their republicratic rule-by-wealth mentality, is now increasing by nearly two billion dollars each and every day. This unspoken reality of undeclared bankruptcy makes it obvious, We, the People, must have a more equitable solution.

Do we have a choice? Yes, as cold and hard as it may sound, we can tell the Congressional republicrats to comply with Article 1, Sec. 8 of the U.S. Constitution, print the money and pay off their-debt.

Eliminating the cost of compounding interest on their debt will help in balancing the budget, and provide a fiscally sound foundation for the construction of our America. On this day of financial atonement, the adjustment will be proportionately distributed among the current holders of every American dollar. If you're already living on next week's paycheck, you won't notice a thing. For the very wealthy, there will be an appropriate correction.

Epilogue

A Time to Begin

Should the nation's priority be on our humanity or Wall Street profits? To answer the question fairly, we must first choose between democracy and plutocracy. Should we reach for a sustainable society, or continue on our current course, an inevitable economic collapse? Your individual answer is critical to the collective future of what could be our-America.

Limited only by our willingness to act, We, the People, must begin the construction of our America. Capitalized by no interest government loans and secured by employee investment and sweat equity, all new business ventures must be exclusively owned and operated by local residents. Infusions of public capital (i.e. grants, subsidies, or rebates,) into the private world of business should still be available as an incentive, but paid back in full, as any responsible investment revenue would be.

Existing corporations financially restructured by modified (debt for equity) Employee Stock Ownership Plans, must return human dignity to every employee, a giant step toward equitable equality. Structured by existing laws and new legislation to create a Capital Homestead Act… We the People, will both create and equitably distribute a new round of American wealth.

The-truth is, individuals must own the houses they live in, and all franchises and commercial facilities must be community owned by resident consumer-taxpayers. In fact, interest-free financing of occupant-owned basic housing would be a needed wealth-creating shot in the nation's economic arm, a right thing to do.

If we can agree, there must be political accountability for the social connection between our needs for basic survival and the greed of rule by wealth, we must ask the primordial question. Who is now deciding which child will be born to purposely endure the inequities of poverty, while another is entitled to the proverbial silver spoon, an unlimited life of leisure?

Allow me to repeat my theory: The dignity-of-ownership is the genesis of all value. Dissolving the barrier between our creation and their possession means, if I made it, I own it, and only I should decide what I would do with it. But, for such an expression to be accurate and enforceable, we must first have - Democratism- a more democratic capitalism, an equal access to knowledge, opportunity, ownership, human dignity, and a sustainable society. With no exceptions, "life, liberty and the pursuit of happiness" must be placed back in the hands of We, the People, where they belong.

"The unexamined life is not worth living."

We must advance beyond the achievements of our parents, or we will be forever restricted by their limitations. Knowledge is the unalterable foundation of life, the connecting link between yesterday's problems and tomorrow's opportunities. But remember this, we are only smarter than our ancestors were because they had the foresight to build schools, libraries, and universities. They trained teachers, and they planned for the future, should we do any less?

Behind political threats of increased taxes, too many Americans are now being denied an equal access to knowledge, the means of success. Building more prisons than schools, to incarcerate their mistakes, is not the way to end rule-by-wealth, the source and cause of this nation's social problems.

The-truth is, as individuals, we are a direct result of growing up in a world of vast wealth and expanding poverty, where grab and greed is the primary path to success. To change this outcome we must do more than merely exist, we must aspire, inspire, and perspire. These natural abilities, within all of us, are yearning to be free, release them and we will free our America from their-government, and, we will free ourselves from subservience to rule by wealth.

This nation's educational system, from kindergarten to college, must become a primary source of personal empowerment, readily available and free to every competent and qualified citizen. We need to teach by subject rather than by a chronological grade system. Let each student learn reading, writing, math and the sciences in a progressive sequence, at a pace that will accommodate each student's ability, and not penalize their shortcomings. We need a quality and quantity of education that will advance all knowledge and not restrict any opportunities.

Regardless of skin color or school tie, to waste any mind is a travesty against the entire population of our America. The threat of increased taxes must never again be used to deter or hinder the human dignity of people.

What is best, not who is right.

Democratism, the best alternative for a stable majority, will restore our America. Three principles must guide We, the People, and the leaders we will choose.

First, we must settle the question of ideology: What should be America's governing philosophy, the plutocracy we have or the democracy we need? The truth is, special interests have corrupted the nation's political system, and minority interests have further weakened our majority rights in a seemingly endless search for retribution. Under the Republicrats, too many middle-class families, and the communities they live in, are being written off, politically devalued by the social and economic pressures of ever-increasing wealth for the rich, and ever more poverty for the poor.

Second, we must settle the moral and ethical choice of people or profit. Which should have the nation's priority? Should corporate profit be allowed to deny our humanity? The-truth is, we need governing representatives who will deliver an equitable human equality and a sustainable quality of life. Rule-by-wealth must end; every American must have free and equal access to knowledge, opportunity and ownership. Our human dignity, now withheld by Wall Street from so many, must be returned through employee ownership in every business and industry.

Third, we must ecologically return to the power of We, the People. Under rule by wealth the nation's forests are being clear-cut without adequate reforestation; too many lakes and rivers are still an abomination of slime and pollution. America, once green and bright is being gouged, paved over, and sold out. We must end this wanton destruction of our natural resources. Please! Don't force our children to regret their parents.

Democratism, once in place, will release many of our scientists, engineers, and hands-on craftsmen from the waste of all price-fixed commercialism. Encouraged to pursue all areas of the unknown, new discoveries will answer many of the what-if questions of the world — inspiring an atmosphere of common-unity — our America focused on what is best, not who is right.

The Constitution of the United States of America

Democratism is crucial to the future of our-America. Only through its democratic institutions can we establish the true character of our existence. By putting humanity before profit we will make the change from rule-by-wealth to rule-by-rights, the natural next step, and it was woven into the fabric of our nation's heritage by the Founders choice of their first three words, We, the People.

The big question is should a Constitutional Convention be called? Article V. states, "The Congress, whenever two-thirds of both Houses shall deem it necessary, shall propose Amendments to the Constitution, or, on application of the legislatures of two-thirds of the several States, shall call a convention for proposing amendments to this Constitution."

Should what-is, be replaced with what-ought to be? The answer is yes!

We, the People, must reach out for political representation without economic corruption. As the sole source and substance of the energy that maintains our Constitution, it must in turn nurture, conserve, and sustain us. Whenever our governing representatives or We, the People, fail in any way to meet our mutual responsibilities, the opportunity to act against the offending party must naturally come into play.

But to even speak of change raises a question of how much change in the existing political corruption and economic greed do we need? Should we accept a small say 25% improvement and leave 75% still corrupt? Or, should we completely replace these republicrats and start all over? Democratism can provide a new beginning, the end must come from We, the People.